YOUNG at HEART
QUILTS

YOUNG at HEA

15 Designs with Color and Style

RT QUILTS

JULIE POPA

Martingale®
& C O M P A N Y

Young at Heart Quilts: 15 Designs with Color and Style
© 2007 by Julie Popa

That Patchwork Place® is an imprint of Martingale & Company®.

Martingale & Company
20205 144th Ave. NE
Woodinville, WA 98072-8478 USA
www.martingale-pub.com

Printed in China
12 11 10 09 08 07   8 7 6 5 4 3 2 1

Library of Congress Cataloging-in-Publication Data
Library of Congress Control Number: 2007001178

ISBN: 978-1-56477-681-5

Mission Statement

Dedicated to providing quality products and service to inspire creativity.

Credits

President & CEO   *Tom Wierzbicki*
Publisher   *Jane Hamada*
Editorial Director   *Mary V. Green*
Managing Editor   *Tina Cook*
Technical Editor   *Laurie Baker*
Copy Editor   *Liz McGehee*
Design Director   *Stan Green*
Illustrator   *Adrienne Smitke*
Cover Designer   *Stan Green*
Text Designer   *Trina Craig*
Photographer   *Brent Kane*

Dedication

To my family: Sean, Shanae, Alexis, Jaclyn, and Stockton.
I love you!

Acknowledgments

My thanks to:

My family for all your patience and love through this.

Paula Murray, you did it again! Thanks for making each quilt come to life with a unique style of its own.

Tina, Amanda, Nicole, Danielle, and Tyler Fonnesbeck for helping mc finish the projects and for entertaining the kids.

My mom and dad, Paul and Yvonne Fonnesbeck, for all of their continued love and support.

CONTENTS

Introduction ～ 8

General Instructions ～ 10

Finishing Techniques ～ 16

QUILTS

    Flirtation ～ 18

    Electric Attitude ～ 24

    Brickwork ～ 29

    School Spirit ～ 33

    Stripes ～ 38

    Tropical Punch ～ 42

    Labyrinth ～ 47

    Vertigo ～ 51

    Zigzag ～ 57

    Cherry Blossoms ～ 61

    Secret Garden ～ 66

    City Streets ～ 72

    Starlight ～ 75

    Twist and Turn ～ 81

    Reflection ～ 85

Gallery of Quilts ～ 89

About the Author ～ 95

INTRODUCTION

My goal for this book was to create a variety of fun, simple, and fast projects that would appeal to teenagers, but I quickly found out that a much broader age group also enjoyed them.

Color plays an important role in all of these quilts. As you scan through the photos of the projects, you'll see that I've used lots of bright hues with a few subtle colorways thrown in, but any of the projects can easily take on a different feel if you substitute fabrics in different colors and tones. Many of the colors were chosen specifically to appeal to a guy or girl, but that too can easily be changed by choosing different colors. Just pick a theme for your quilt and keep the colors and fabrics consistent with the finished look you desire, and you'll end up with a great quilt.

If you are making a project for a younger recipient, I encourage you to include him or her in the fabric-selection process as well as the sewing. Many of the projects are easy enough for a beginning quilter to make, while others can be accomplished with a little help from a more experienced sewer. My teenage nieces helped sew several of the projects in this book and had a great time doing it. Age is no barrier when it comes to quilting, whether you're making the quilt or just enjoying it. Have fun!

GENERAL INSTRUCTIONS

This section will serve as a quick overview of the techniques needed to make the projects in this book. If you are new to quilting, I suggest you invest in a book that covers the basic techniques in depth, such as *The Quilter's Quick Reference Guide* by Candace Eisner Strick (Martingale & Company, 2004), and take a beginning quilting class from your local quilt shop if possible.

Rotary Cutting

All the pieces for the quilts in this book were cut using rotary-cutting techniques. Strips are cut across the width of the fabric first, and then squares and rectangles are cut from the strips. Triangles are created by cutting squares in half once or twice diagonally.

1. Fold the fabric in half lengthwise, wrong sides together, with the selvages matching. Lay the fabric on a rotary-cutting mat with the folded edge toward you.

Selvages

Fold

2. Place the edge of a square ruler along the folded edge. Then lay a 6½" x 24" ruler to the left of the square ruler. Position the long ruler so that it covers both cut edges of the fabric.

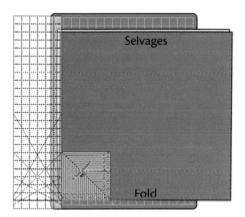

3. Remove the square ruler and cut along the long edge of the ruler on the right-hand side. Discard the cut piece.

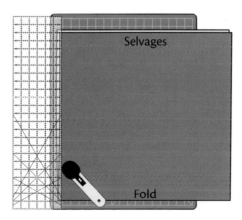

4. Measuring from the straightened edge, cut strips to the width given in the pattern instructions.

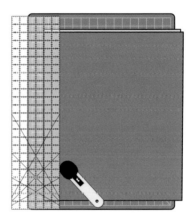

5. To cut squares and rectangles, lay a folded strip on the mat with the selvage ends to the right. Straighten the selvage ends by aligning a horizontal line of the ruler with the long edge of the folded strip in the same manner as for the whole fabric piece. Place the straightened edge to your left and then measure the required distance from the end of the strip to cut your pieces.

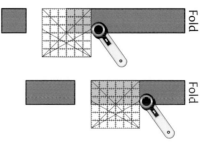

6. If the project instructions indicate to cut squares in half diagonally, align the edge of your ruler diagonally from corner to corner on each square and cut. This will create two half-square triangles.

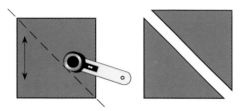

If the project instructions tell you to cut squares twice diagonally, make the first cut as above. Without disturbing the pieces, align your ruler diagonally from one remaining un-cut corner to the other uncut corner, and make the second cut. This will create four quarter-square triangles.

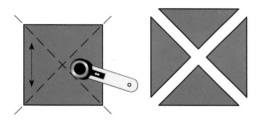

Making and Using Templates

Two of the projects, "Flirtation" and "Zigzag," will require you to use templates to cut pieces for the blocks.

To make a template, choose one of the following methods:
*   Trace the pattern onto template plastic using a fine-point permanent marker. Transfer the template letter and grain-line arrow to the pattern. Cut out the shape on the marked line.
*   Photocopy the pattern and roughly cut it out. Glue the pattern to a manila folder or heavy card stock and then follow the line to cut it out.

To cut out the pieces using the template, place the template, right side up, on the right side of a single layer of the fabric indicated, following the grain-line arrow. Trace around the template with a sharp pencil. Trace as many shapes as needed and then use scissors to cut out the pieces on the marked lines.

To cut reversed pieces, simply turn the template over and trace from the wrong side. If both regular and reversed pieces are needed, place the template on a double layer of fabric with wrong sides together, trace around it, and cut out the shapes. The top shape will be the regular piece, and the bottom shape will be the reversed piece.

Tips for Cutting with Templates

When cutting patchwork pieces using a template, I find it easier to cut the pieces from fabric strips whenever possible. To do this, I measure the widest part of the template and cut a strip to that width from the appropriate fabric. The above instructions can then be used to trace and cut out the pieces.

For templates with straight edges, instead of tracing around the template, I lay my ruler along the edge of the template and then rotary cut along the ruler edge. Be careful not to move the piece as you cut it out to ensure an accurate piece.

Adding Borders

All the quilts in this book use the butted-corner method, which is the easiest to do. Most of the borders are longer than the fabric width, which will require you to piece the strips together and then trim them to the required lengths. If you prefer borders that are not pieced, cut the strips to the needed length from the lengthwise grain of the fabric. This usually requires more fabric, but the border will be more stable.

1. Using a diagonal seam, sew the strips together end to end to make one long strip as shown. A diagonal seam is stronger and less noticeable than a straight seam. Trim the extra fabric at each seam, leaving a ¼" seam allowance. Press the seam allowance open.

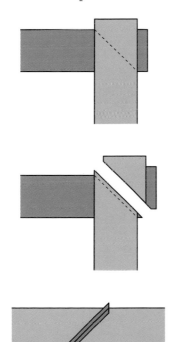

2. Measure the quilt top through the center from top to bottom and cut two border strips to that measurement. Sew the strips to the sides of the quilt top. Press the seam allowances toward the border strips.

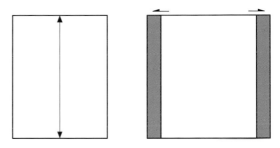

Measure the vertical center.

3. Measure the quilt through the center from side to side, including the borders that you just added. Cut two strips to that measurement. Sew the strips to the top and bottom of the quilt top. Press the seam allowances toward the border strips.

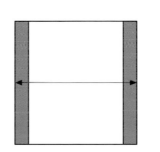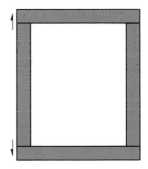

Measure the horizontal center.

Fusible-Web Appliqué

Using your preferred paper-backed fusible-web product, refer to the following steps to create perfect fusible-appliqué shapes.

1. Using the pattern(s) provided with the project, trace the appliqué shapes with a pencil onto the paper side of the fusible web. Trace each shape as many times as needed for your chosen project, leaving about ½" between shapes. (Shapes that are not symmetrical have already been reversed so that the finished image will be correct.)

2. Cut out each shape roughly ¼" outside the drawn lines.

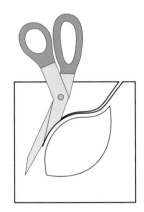

3. To prevent larger shapes from becoming too stiff and heavy for your finished quilted project, cut out the center of the paper shape ¼" from the drawn line.

4. Follow the manufacturer's instructions to fuse the shapes to the wrong side of the fabric indicated on the pattern. Allow the shapes to cool and then cut out each appliqué shape on the drawn line.

Fabric
(wrong side up)

5. Remove the paper backing from the appliqué shapes. Refer to the project photo as well as any diagrams to position the shapes on the background fabric. Fuse the shapes in placc.

6. To secure the edges, machine stitch around the edge of each appliqué shape with matching thread. Use a blanket stitch for a traditional look or a narrow zigzag for a more contemporary look.

Blanket stitch   Zigzag stitch

FINISHING TECHNIQUES

This section highlights the steps needed to finish your quilt. If you need further instruction, please consult a good technique book.

Layering and Basting

Before you can quilt your project, it must be layered with the batting and backing and then basted together. You will need batting and backing pieces that are 3" to 4" larger than your quilt top on each side. For the projects in this book, you will need to cut and piece your backing fabric so it is large enough. Press the seams open.

1. Lay out your backing, wrong side up, on a flat surface. Tape or pin down the edges so that the backing is taut but not stretched.

2. Center the batting over the backing and smooth it out.

3. Center the quilt top, right side up, over the batting so that the edges are parallel with the edges of the backing. Smooth out any wrinkles.

4. Baste the quilt layers together using 1"-long rustproof safety pins. Begin pinning in the center of the quilt, working your way out toward the edges. Place pins every 3" to 4".

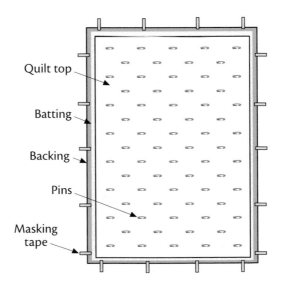

Quilt top

Batting

Backing

Pins

Masking tape

Binding

I use 2½"-wide straight-grain strips, cut across the width of the fabric, to bind my projects.

1. Cut the number of strips specified in the project instructions, and sew the strips together end to end using a diagonal seam (refer to "Adding Borders" on page 13). Trim the seam to ¼" and press open.

2. Cut one end of the binding strip at a 45° angle. Press under the angled end ¼" to the wrong side. With wrong sides together, fold the strip in half lengthwise; press.

3. Place the raw edges of the binding even with the raw edges of the quilt, starting at the center of the bottom edge. Start sewing 3" from the beginning of the binding strip. Sew the binding to the quilt using a ¼" seam allowance. Stop sewing ¼" from the first corner; backstitch. Remove the quilt from the machine.

4. Rotate the quilt so that you will be ready to sew the next edge. Fold the binding strip up so that the edge of the strip is even with the edge of the quilt; then fold the strip down, keeping the fold even with the edge of the quilt. Begin sewing at the edge and continue until you are ¼" from the next corner. Repeat this step at each corner.

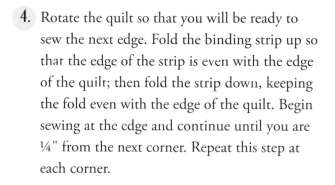

5. Stitch around the entire quilt, stopping about 6" from where you began. Remove the quilt from your machine. Overlap the end of the binding with the beginning. Trim the end of the binding so it extends at least ¼" past the beginning of the strip. Tuck the end of the binding into the beginning end of the binding, and finish sewing the binding to the quilt.

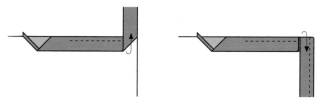

6. Turn the binding over to the back of the quilt so it covers the stitching. Blindstitch it in place, mitering the corners.

FLIRTATION

By Julie Popa. Quilted by Paula Murray.

Raw-edge appliqué and chenille fabric give this quilt a very country feel, which contrasts with the elegant floral design and the hourglass curve to create a beautiful "shabby chic" look.

Finished Quilt: 64½" x 88½"
Finished Block: 13" x 19"

Materials

Yardages are based on 42"-wide fabrics unless otherwise noted.

- 3⅜ yards of 52"-wide white chenille for blocks
- 3⅓ yards *total* of assorted cream prints for block backgrounds
- 1½ yards of cream-and-tan plaid for border
- 1⅓ yards of green print for stem and leaf appliqués
- ⅞ yard of tan floral print for block corners
- ⅜ yard of dark pink print for flower appliqués
- ¼ yard of light pink print for flower-center appliqués
- ⅛ yard of medium pink print for flower-bud appliqués
- ⅔ yard of fabric for binding
- 5⅞ yards of fabric for backing
- 72" x 96" piece of batting
- 4½ yards of 17"-wide paper-backed fusible web

Cutting

All measurements include ¼"-wide seam allowances. Cut all strips across the width of the fabric. Before you begin cutting, refer to "Making and Using Templates" on page 12 to make templates A and B from the patterns on page 23, and use them to cut out the indicated pieces.

From the assorted cream prints, cut a *total* of:
16 rectangles, 13½" x 19½"

From the white chenille, cut:
32 template A pieces

From the tan floral print, cut:
32 template B pieces
32 template B reversed pieces

From the cream-and-tan plaid, cut:
7 strips, 6½" x 42"

From the binding fabric, cut:
8 strips, 2½" x 42"

Making the Blocks

1. With the straight edges aligned, pin two chenille template A pieces onto each assorted cream background rectangle as shown. Sew the A pieces in place, ¼" from the curved edges.

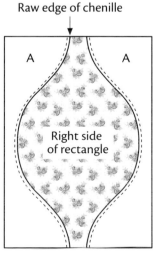

Raw edge of chenille

A   A

Right side
of rectangle

Make 16.

2. Pin two template B and two template B reversed pieces in the corners of each rectangle, aligning the straight edges. Sew ¼" from the curved edges of each B piece as shown.

Raw edge

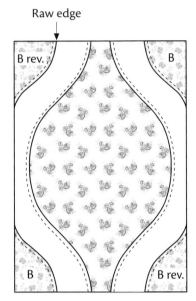

3. Using the patterns on page 22, refer to "Fusible-Web Appliqué" on page 14 to make the appliqués from the fabrics specified on the patterns, trimming away the excess fusible web from the center of the fusible-web flower shapes before adhering them to the dark pink fabric.

4. Position the appliqués on each step 2 rectangle as shown. Follow the manufacturer's instructions to fuse the appliqués in place.

5. Machine blanket-stitch around the edges of the appliqué shapes to secure them in place.

6. Square up each block. Turn each block over to the wrong side and cut away the background fabric under the template A pieces, leaving a ¼" seam allowance. Cut away the background fabric and the chenille fabric under each template B piece, leaving a ¼" seam allowance. Be careful not to cut into the top fabrics.

Assembling the Quilt Top

1. Arrange the blocks in four horizontal rows of four blocks each. Sew the blocks into rows. Press the seam allowances in opposite directions from row to row. Sew the rows together. Press the seam allowances in either direction.

2. Sew the plaid strips together end to end and press the seam allowances to one side. Refer to "Adding Borders" on page 13 to cut and sew the border.

Finishing the Quilt

Refer to "Finishing Techniques" on page 16 to layer and baste your quilt, and quilt as desired. Prepare the binding and sew it to the quilt edges.

To vary the quilt design, make a different template that creates a circular opening; then fill the opening with an appliqué design of your choice.

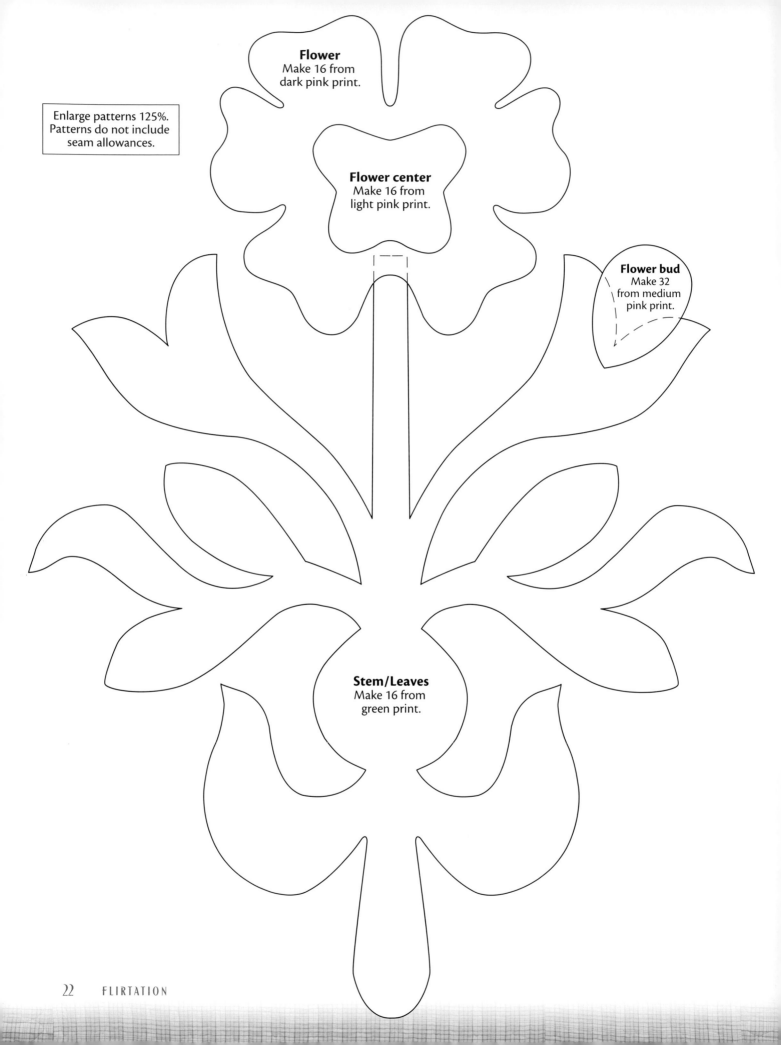

Flower
Make 16 from
dark pink print.

Enlarge patterns 125%.
Patterns do not include
seam allowances.

Flower center
Make 16 from
light pink print.

Flower bud
Make 32
from medium
pink print.

Stem/Leaves
Make 16 from
green print.

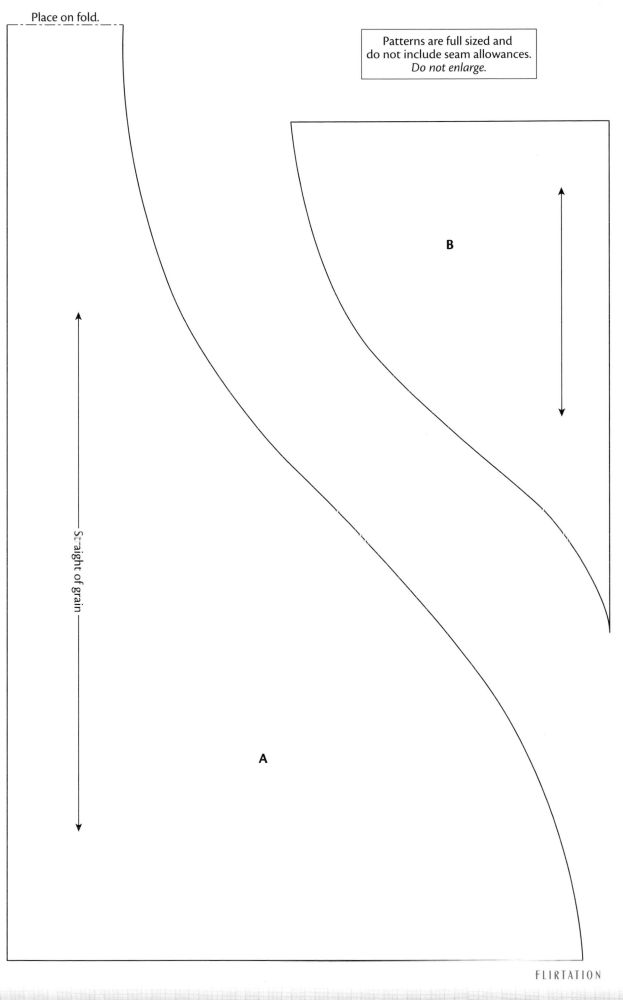

Place on fold.

Patterns are full sized and
do not include seam allowances.
Do not enlarge.

B

Straight of grain

A

ELECTRIC ATTITUDE

By Julie Popa. Quilted by Paula Murray.

Get your attitude charged with this lively quilt! Quick and easy piecing techniques make this project go together fast.

FINISHED QUILT: 58½" x 82½"
FINISHED BLOCK: 8½" x 8½"

Materials

Yardages are based on 42"-wide fabrics.

- ⅓ yard *each* of dark purple, teal, dark brown, sage, pumpkin, gold, lilac, mustard, and rust solids for Chain blocks
- 2½ yards of black solid for Chain blocks, Nine Patch–in-a-Square blocks, corner setting triangles, and border
- 1⅜ yards of bright multicolored print for Square-in-a-Square blocks, Nine Patch–in-a-Square blocks, and side setting triangles
- ⅞ yard of red solid for Chain blocks, Nine Patch–in-a-Square blocks, and side setting triangles
- ⅝ yard of very dark purple solid for Square-in-a-Square blocks
- ⅔ yards of fabric for binding
- 5½ yards of fabric for backing
- 66" x 90" piece of batting

Cutting

All measurements include ¼"-wide seam allowances. Cut all strips across the width of the fabric.

From the black solid, cut:

14 strips, 2" x 42"
2 strips, 3½" x 42"
8 strips, 5½" x 42"
2 squares, 6½" x 6½"; cut in half diagonally to yield 4 triangles

From the dark purple solid, cut:

1 strip, 2" x 42"
3 squares, 5⅛" x 5⅛"; cut in half diagonally to yield 6 triangles
6 squares, 3½" x 3½"

From *each* of the teal, dark brown, sage, pumpkin, and gold solids, cut:

1 strip, 2" x 42" (6 total)
3 squares, 5⅛" x 5⅛" (18 total); cut in half diagonally to yield 6 triangles (36 total; 1 of each color left over)
5 squares, 3½" x 3½" (30 total)

From *each* of the lilac, mustard, and rust solids, cut:

1 strip, 2" x 42" (3 total)
2 squares, 5⅛" x 5⅛" (6 total); cut in half diagonally to yield 4 triangles (12 total)
4 squares, 3½" x 3½" (12 total)

From the red solid, cut:

3 strips, 3½" x 42"; crosscut 1 strip into 5 squares, 3½" x 3½"
5 strips, 2" x 42"
3 squares, 5⅛" x 5⅛"; cut in half diagonally to yield 6 triangles (1 left over)

From the bright multicolored print, cut:

2 squares, 13¼" x 13¼"; cut twice diagonally to yield 8 triangles (2 left over)
5 squares, 5½" x 5½"; cut twice diagonally to yield 20 triangles
35 squares, 5⅛" x 5⅛"; cut in half diagonally to yield 70 triangles

Continued on page 26

Continued from page 25

From the very dark purple solid, cut:

8 squares, 6½" x 6½"

From the binding fabric, cut:

8 strips, 2½" x 42"

Making the Blocks

1. To make the Chain blocks, sew a black 2" x 42" strip to each dark purple, teal, dark brown, sage, pumpkin, gold, lilac, mustard, and rust solid 2" x 42" strip and one red solid 2" x 42" strip along the long edges to make a strip set (10 strip sets total). Press the seam allowances away from the black strips. Crosscut the dark purple strip set into 12 segments, 2" wide. Crosscut the teal, dark brown, sage, pumpkin, gold, and red strip sets into 10 segments, 2" wide. Crosscut the lilac, mustard, and rust strip sets into 8 segments, 2" wide. You should have a total of 96 segments.

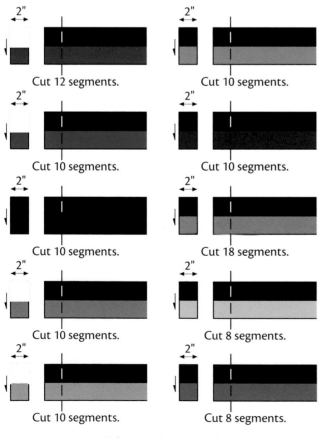

Cut 12 segments.   Cut 10 segments.

Cut 10 segments.   Cut 10 segments.

Cut 10 segments.   Cut 18 segments.

Cut 10 segments.   Cut 8 segments.

Cut 10 segments.   Cut 8 segments.

Make 10 strip sets total.

2. Referring to the quilt photo on page 24 or the diagram on page 28 for color pairings, sew a segment from one strip set to a segment from a different-colored strip set to make a four-patch unit. Press the seam allowances in either direction. Make another four-patch unit using the same color combination. Make a total of 24 pairs of four-patch units.

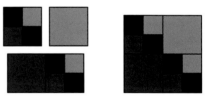

Make 24 pairs.

3. Arrange two matching four-patch units and one 3½" square from each of the two colors used in the four-patch units as shown. Be careful to orient the black squares so they form a diagonal line. Sew the pieces together to make the center square. Repeat with the remaining four-patch units and 3½" squares.

Make 24.

4. Using two 5⅛" triangles that match each of the 3½" squares of the center square, sew one of each color triangle to opposite sides of a center square, being sure that the triangles are on the same side as the matching color square. Press the seam allowances toward the triangles. Sew the remaining triangles to the top and bottom of the center square, again being sure that the triangle is on the same side as the matching square. Press the seam allowances

toward the triangles. Repeat with the remaining center squares to make 24 Chain blocks.

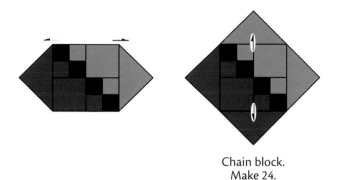

Chain block.
Make 24.

5. To make the Square-in-a-Square blocks, sew a multicolored 5⅛" triangle to opposite sides of each very dark purple 6½" square. Press the seam allowances toward the triangles. Repeat with the top and bottom edges of the squares to make eight blocks.

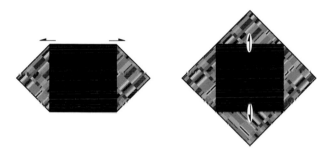

Square-in-a-Square block.
Make 8.

6. To make the Nine Patch–in-a-Square blocks, sew a red 2" x 42" strip to each side of a black 3½" x 42" strip to make a strip set. Make two. Press the seam allowances toward the black strips. Crosscut the strip sets into 7 segments, 3½" wide, and 10 segments, 2" wide.

3½" 2"

Make 2 strip sets.
Cut 7 segments, 3½" wide.
Cut 10 segments, 2" wide.

7. Sew a black 2" x 42" strip to each side of a red 3½" x 42" strip to make a strip set. Make two. Press the seam allowances toward the black strips. Crosscut the strip sets into 24 segments, 2" wide.

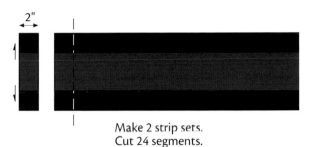

2"

Make 2 strip sets.
Cut 24 segments.

8. Sew one 3½" segment from step 6 and two segments from step 7 together as shown to make a nine-patch unit. Make seven. Set aside the remaining segments from steps 6 and 7 for the pieced side setting triangles.

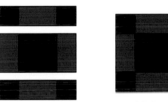

Make 7.

9. Sew a multicolored 5⅛" triangle to opposite sides of each nine-patch unit. Press the seam allowances toward the triangles. Repeat with the remaining sides.

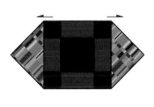
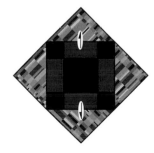

Make 7.

Making the Pieced Side Setting Triangles

1. Using the leftover strip-set segments from "Making the Blocks," sew the segments together as shown. Make 10. Press the seam allowances in either direction.

Make 10.

2. Sew a multicolored 5½" triangle to the sides of each step 1 unit. Press the seam allowances toward the triangles. Add a multicolored 5⅛" triangle to the top of each unit. Press the seam allowances toward the triangles.

Make 10.

Assembling the Quilt Top

1. Arrange the blocks, pieced side setting triangles, multicolored 13¼" side setting triangles, and black corner setting triangles in diagonal rows as shown. Be careful to orient the Chain blocks so that the black squares form diagonal lines across the quilt top. Sew the blocks and side setting triangles into rows. Press the seam allowances in opposite directions from row to row. Sew the rows together and then add the corner triangles.

2. Sew the black 5½" x 42" strips together end to end and press the seam allowances to one side. Refer to "Adding Borders" on page 13 to cut and sew the border.

Finishing the Quilt

Refer to "Finishing Techniques" on page 16 to layer and baste your quilt, and quilt as desired. Prepare the binding and sew it to the quilt edges.

BRICKWORK

Designed by Julie Popa. Sewn by Amanda Fonnesbeck, age 16, and Nicole Fonnesbeck, age 15 .
Quilted by Paula Murray.

This is such a fun quilt! The fabrics and the strong horizontal lines give it a very casual, beachy feel. My nieces sewed this quilt for me. It was Amanda's second quilt and Nicole's first. They did a great job!

FINISHED QUILT: 60½" x 83"
FINISHED BLOCK: 7½" x 20"

Materials

Yardages are based on 42"-wide fabrics.
4 yards *total* of assorted prints for blocks
1⅞ yards of blue print for background pieces
    and border
⅔ yard of fabric for binding
5½ yards of fabric for backing
68" x 90" piece of batting

Cutting

All measurements include ¼"-wide seam allowances. Cut all strips across the width of the fabric unless otherwise noted.

From the blue print, cut:
2 strips, 8" x 62", along the *lengthwise* grain
10 rectangles, 8" x 10½"

From the binding fabric, cut:
8 strips, 2½" x 42"

For block A, repeat the following cutting instructions five times, using different print combinations.

From 1 of the assorted prints, cut:
1 rectangle, 3" x 10½", for the center

From a different assorted print, cut:
2 rectangles, 3" x 10½", for the outer top and
    bottom
2 rectangles, 5½" x 8", for the outer sides

For block B, repeat the following cutting instructions seven times, using different print combinations.

From 1 of the assorted prints, cut:
1 rectangle, 2" x 14½", for the center

From a different assorted print, cut:
2 rectangles, 2½" x 14½", for the inner top and
    bottom
2 rectangles, 2½" x 6", for the inner sides

From another assorted print, cut:
2 rectangles, 1½" x 18½", for the outer top and
    bottom
2 rectangles, 1½" x 8", for the outer sides

For block C, repeat the following cutting instructions 10 times, using different print combinations.

From 1 of the assorted prints, cut:
1 rectangle, 4" x 16½", for the center

From a different assorted print, cut:
2 rectangles, 2½" x 16½", for the outer top and
    bottom
2 rectangles, 2½" x 8", for the outer sides

Making the Blocks

1. To make block A, sew matching outer top/bottom rectangles to each side of a center rectangle as shown. Make five. Press the seam allowances away from the center.

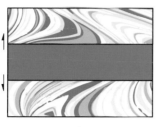

Make 5.

2. Sew the outer side rectangles that match the outer top/bottom rectangles to the sides of each step 1 unit to complete the blocks. Press the seam allowances toward the side rectangles.

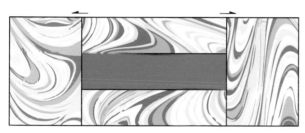

Block A.
Make 5.

3. To make block B, sew matching inner top/bottom rectangles to each side of a center rectangle. Make seven. Press the seam allowances away from the center.

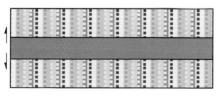

Make 7.

4. Sew the inner side rectangles that match the inner top/bottom rectangles to the sides of each step 3 unit. Press the seam allowances away from the center.

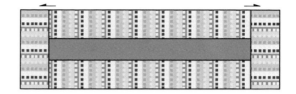

5. Add matching outer top/bottom rectangles and then matching outer side rectangles to each step 4 unit to complete the blocks. Press the seam allowances away from the center after each addition.

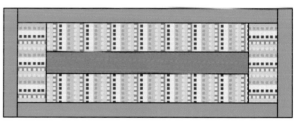

Block B
Make 7.

6. To make block C, sew matching outer top/bottom rectangles to each side of a center rectangle. Make 10. Press the seam allowances away from the center.

Make 10.

7. Sew the outer side rectangles that match the outer top/bottom rectangles to the sides of each step 6 unit to complete the blocks. Press the seam allowances away from the center.

Block C.
Make 10.

Assembling the Quilt Top

1. Arrange the blocks and blue 8" x 10½" rectangles into nine horizontal rows as shown. The blocks can be rearranged from row to row, if desired, but the number of blocks in each row must remain the same. Sew the blocks and rectangles into rows. Press the seam allowances in either direction. Sew the rows together. Press the seam allowances in either direction.

2. Refer to "Adding Borders" on page 13 to trim the blue 8" x 62" strips to the correct lengths for the top and bottom borders and sew them to the quilt top. Press the seam allowances toward the border.

Finishing the Quilt

Refer to "Finishing Techniques" on page 16 to layer and baste your quilt, and quilt as desired. Prepare the binding and sew it to the quilt edges.

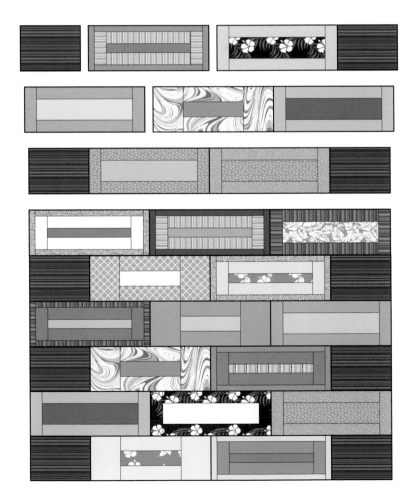

School Spirit

By Julie Popa. Quilted by Paula Murray.

No matter what your age, team spirit never goes out of style. Personalize this quilt with colors from your high school or favorite sports team.

Finished Quilt: 64½" x 82½"
Finished Block: 9" x 9"

Materials

Yardages are based on 42"-wide fabrics.

2¾ yards of dark purple print for blocks, appliqué, and border

2 yards of light purple print for blocks, appliqué, and binding

1⅓ yards of dark yellow print for blocks and appliqué

1⅓ yards of light yellow print for blocks and appliqué

1⅛ yards of white print for blocks

4 yards of fabric for backing

72" x 90" piece of batting

1⅝ yards of 17"-wide paper-backed fusible web

Cutting

*All measurements include ¼"-wide seam allowances.
Cut all strips across the width of the fabric.*

From the white print, cut:
48 strips, 1½" x 15"

From the dark purple print, cut:
6 squares, 9⅞" x 9⅞"; cut in half diagonally to yield 12 triangles
6 squares, 8⅜" x 8⅜"; cut in half diagonally to yield 12 triangles
8 strips, 5½" x 42"

From the light purple print, cut:
6 squares, 9⅞" x 9⅞"; cut in half diagonally to yield 12 triangles
6 squares, 8⅜" x 8⅜"; cut in half diagonally to yield 12 triangles
8 strips, 2½" x 42"

From the dark yellow print, cut:
6 squarcs, 9⅞" x 9⅞"; cut in half diagonally to yield 12 triangles
6 squares, 8⅜" x 8⅜"; cut in half diagonally to yield 12 triangles

From the light yellow print, cut:
6 squares, 9⅞" x 9⅞"; cut in half diagonally to yield 12 triangles
6 squares, 8⅜" x 8⅜"; cut in half diagonally to yield 12 triangles

Making the Blocks

1. Center and sew a white strip to the long edge of each dark purple, light purple, dark yellow, and light yellow 8⅜" triangle. You will be sewing along the bias edge of the triangles so be careful not to stretch them while sewing. Press the seam allowances toward the triangles. Trim the ends of the strips even with the sides of the triangles.

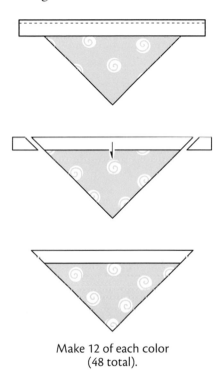

Make 12 of each color
(48 total).

2. Sew a corresponding-color 9⅞" triangle to each step 1 unit. Press the seam allowances toward the triangles.

 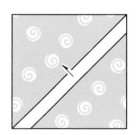

Make 12 of each color
(48 total).

3. Using the patterns on page 37, refer to "Fusible-Web Appliqué" on page 14 to make the appliqués from the remainder of the purple and yellow fabrics as specified on the patterns.

4. With the edges aligned, follow the manufacturer's instructions to position and fuse a dark purple large kite piece in the corner of the 9⅞" triangle side of each dark yellow unit from step 2 as shown; fuse a light purple small kite piece in the opposite corner. Repeat with the remaining step 2 units and large and small kite pieces to make the blocks in the color combinations shown. Always fuse the large kite pieces to the larger triangles of each block and the small kite pieces to the smaller triangles.

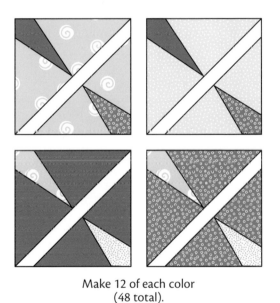

Make 12 of each color
(48 total).

5. Machine zigzag stitch around the edges of the appliqué shapes to secure them in place.

Assembling the Quilt Top

1. Arrange the blocks into eight horizontal rows of six blocks each as shown. Sew the blocks into rows. Press the seam allowances toward the purple blocks. Sew the rows together. Press the seam allowances in either direction.

   NOTE: Be sure to follow the diagram and not the quilt photo; the photo shows a quilt with the rows sewn together differently.

2. Sew the dark purple 5½" x 42" strips together end to end. Press the seam allowances to one side. Refer to "Adding Borders" on page 13 to cut the pieced strip to the lengths needed for the border and sew them to the quilt top. Press the seam allowances toward the border.

Finishing the Quilt

Refer to "Finishing Techniques" on page 16 to layer and baste your quilt, and quilt as desired. Prepare the light purple binding and sew it to the quilt edges.

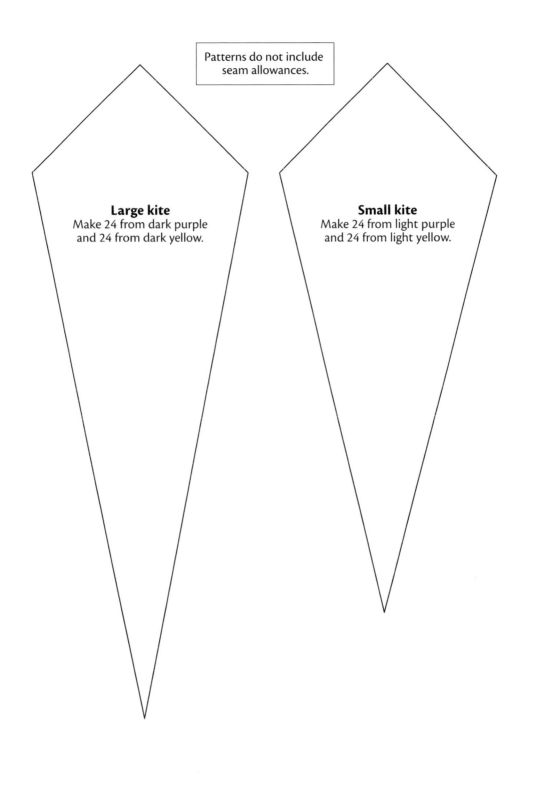

Patterns do not include seam allowances.

Large kite
Make 24 from dark purple and 24 from dark yellow.

Small kite
Make 24 from light purple and 24 from light yellow.

STRIPES

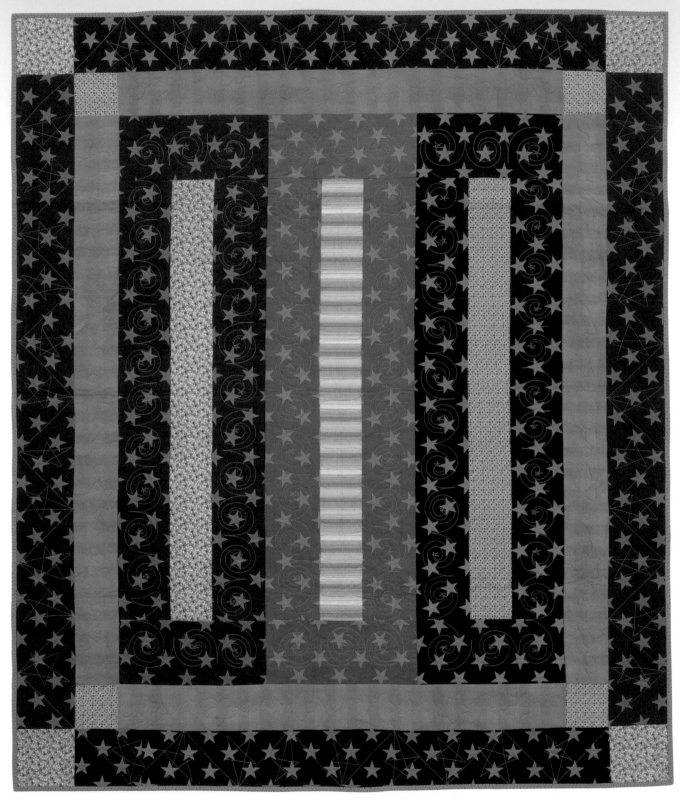

Pieced by Tina Fonnesbeck and Julie Popa. Quilted by Paula Murray.

This quilt is great for a beginner project or a quick gift. The wide strips are perfect for showcasing large novelty and floral prints and the straight lines make the piecing easy. In fact, the most difficult part about this quilt is deciding what fabrics to use.

Finished Quilt: 61½" x 71½"

Materials

Yardages are based on 42"-wide fabrics.

1⅓ yards of dark red print for panels and outer border

1⅓ yards of gold print for inner border and binding

1⅛ yards of black print for panels and outer border

⅝ yard of green print for panels

⅓ yard of off-white print 1 for panels and inner-border corner squares

⅓ yard of off-white print 2 for panels and outer-border corner squares

¼ yard of off-white print 3 for panels

4 yards of fabric for backing

70" x 80" piece of batting

Cutting

All measurements include ¼"-wide seam allowances.
Cut all strips across the width of the fabric.

From the black print, cut:
2 strips, 5½" x 40½"
2 rectangles, 6½" x 14½"
3 strips, 6" x 42"

From the green print, cut:
2 strips, 5½" x 40½"
2 rectangles, 6½" x 14½"

From the dark red print, cut:
2 strips, 5½" x 40½"
2 rectangles, 6½" x 14½"
4 strips, 6" x 42"

From off-white print 1, cut:
1 strip, 4½" x 40½"
4 squares, 4½" x 4½"

From off-white print 2, cut:
1 strip, 4½" x 40½"
4 squares, 6" x 6"

From off-white print 3, cut:
1 strip, 4½" x 40½"

From the gold print, cut:
5 strips, 4½" x 42"
7 strips, 2½" x 42"

Making the Panels

1. Sew matching 5½" x 40½" strips to the sides of each off-white 4½" x 40½" strip. Press the seam allowances away from the off-white strips. Make three.

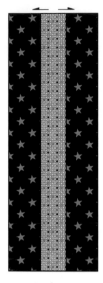

Make 3.

2. Add a 6½" x 14½" rectangle that matches the outer strips to the top and bottom of each step 1 unit to complete the panels. Press the seam allowances toward the rectangles.

Make 3.

Assembling the Quilt Top

1. Sew the panels together along the long edges as shown.

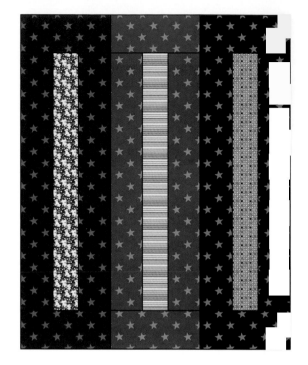

2. Sew the gold 4½" x 42" strips together end to end and press the seam allowances to one side. Refer to "Adding Borders" on page 13 to cut two side borders. Cut two borders for the top and bottom of the quilt, *not* including the measurement of the side borders.

3. Refer to the quilt assembly diagram on page 41 to sew the side borders to the sides of the quilt top. Press the seam allowances toward the border. Join an off-white print 1 square to the ends of the top and bottom borders. Sew the borders to the top and bottom of the quilt top. Press the seam allowances toward the border.

4. Sew the dark red 6" x 42" strips together end to end and press the seam allowances to one side. Refer to "Adding Borders" to cut two outer side borders. Do not sew them to the quilt top yet.

5. Join the black 6" x 42" strips together end to end and press the seam allowances to one side. Refer to "Adding Borders" to cut two borders for the outer top and bottom of the quilt, *not* including the measurement of the side borders. Add an off-white print 2 square to the ends of each strip.

6. Sew the dark red outer side borders to the sides of the quilt top. Sew the black outer top and bottom borders to the top and bottom of the quilt top. Press the seam allowances toward the outer border.

Finishing the Quilt

Refer to "Finishing Techniques" on page 16 to layer and baste your quilt, and quilt as desired. Prepare the gold print binding and sew it to the quilt edges.

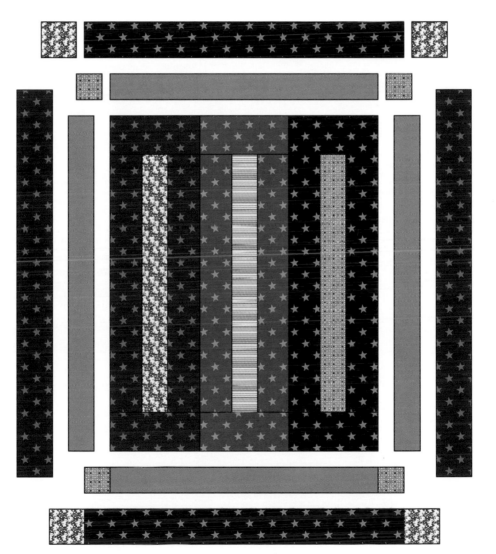

Quilt assembly

TROPICAL PUNCH

By Julie Popa. Quilted by Paula Murray.

Punch up the color in your room with this fun and fast lap quilt. Add more blocks for a bed quilt or make fewer blocks for a great wall hanging.

FINISHED QUILT: 55" x 67"
FINISHED BLOCK: 9½" x 9½"

Materials

Yardages are based on 42"-wide fabrics.

3 yards *total* of assorted bright prints for blocks, flower-petal appliqués, sashing squares, and pieced middle border

1¾ yards of yellow print for sashing and inner and outer borders

⅛ yard of dark yellow for flower-center appliqués

⅝ yard of fabric for binding

3⅞ yards of fabric for backing

63" x 75" piece of batting

3½ yards of 17"-wide paper-backed fusible web

Cutting

All measurements include ¼"-wide seam allowances.
Cut all strips across the width of the fabric.

From the assorted bright prints, cut a *total* of:
12 squares, 10" x 10"
40 squares, 5" x 5"
4 rectangles, 5" x 6½"

From 1 of the assorted bright prints, cut:
6 squares, 3" x 3"

From the yellow print, cut:
17 rectangles, 3" x 10"
5 strips, 4" x 42"
7 strips, 3" x 42"

From the binding fabric, cut:
7 strips, 2½" x 42"

Making the Blocks

1. Using the patterns on page 46, refer to "Fusible-Web Appliqué" on page 14 to make the appliqués from the fabrics specified on the patterns, trimming away the excess fusible web from the center of the fusible-web flower-petal shapes before adhering them to the assorted bright prints.

2. Position each flower-petal appliqué on a bright-print 10" square that is a different print than the appliqué. Place the edges of the appliqués even with the edges of the squares. Follow the manufacturer's instructions to fuse the petal appliqués in place. Fuse the flower-center appliqués to the center of the flower-petal appliqués. Make 12.

Make 12.

3. Machine zigzag stitch around the edges of the appliqué shapes to secure them in place.

Assembling the Quilt Top

1. Sew three blocks and two yellow 3" x 10" sashing rectangles together as shown to make the block rows. Make four. Press the seam allowances toward the sashing.

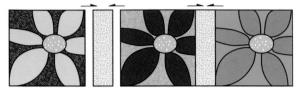

Make 4.

2. Using the remaining yellow sashing rectangles and the 3" squares cut from one bright print, make three sashing rows as shown. Press the seam allowances toward the sashing.

Make 3.

3. Sew the block and sashing rows together as shown. Press the seam allowances toward the sashing rows.

4. Sew the yellow 4" x 42" strips together end to end and press the seam allowances to one side. From the pieced strip, cut two strips, 4" x 46", for the inner side borders, and two strips, 4" x 41", for the inner top and bottom borders. Sew the inner side borders to the sides of the quilt top. Press the seam allowances toward the border. Sew the inner top and bottom borders to the top and bottom of the quilt top. Press the seam allowances toward the border.

5. To make the pieced middle top and bottom borders, refer to the quilt assembly diagram on page 45 to join nine assorted bright-print squares side by side. Press the seam allowances in one direction. Repeat to make one additional pieced border strip. Sew the strips to the top and bottom of the quilt top. Press the seam allowances toward the inner border.

6. To make the pieced middle side borders, join 11 assorted bright squares side by side. Press the seam allowances in one direction. Repeat to make one additional pieced border strip. Add an assorted bright 5" x 6½" rectangle to the ends of each border strip. Sew these strips to the sides of the quilt top. Press the seam allowances toward the inner border.

7. Sew the yellow 3" x 42" strips together end to end and press the seam allowances to one side. Refer to "Adding Borders" on page 13 to cut and sew the outer borders.

Finishing the Quilt

Refer to "Finishing Techniques" on page 16 to layer and baste your quilt, and quilt as desired. Prepare the binding and sew it to the quilt edges.

Quilt assembly

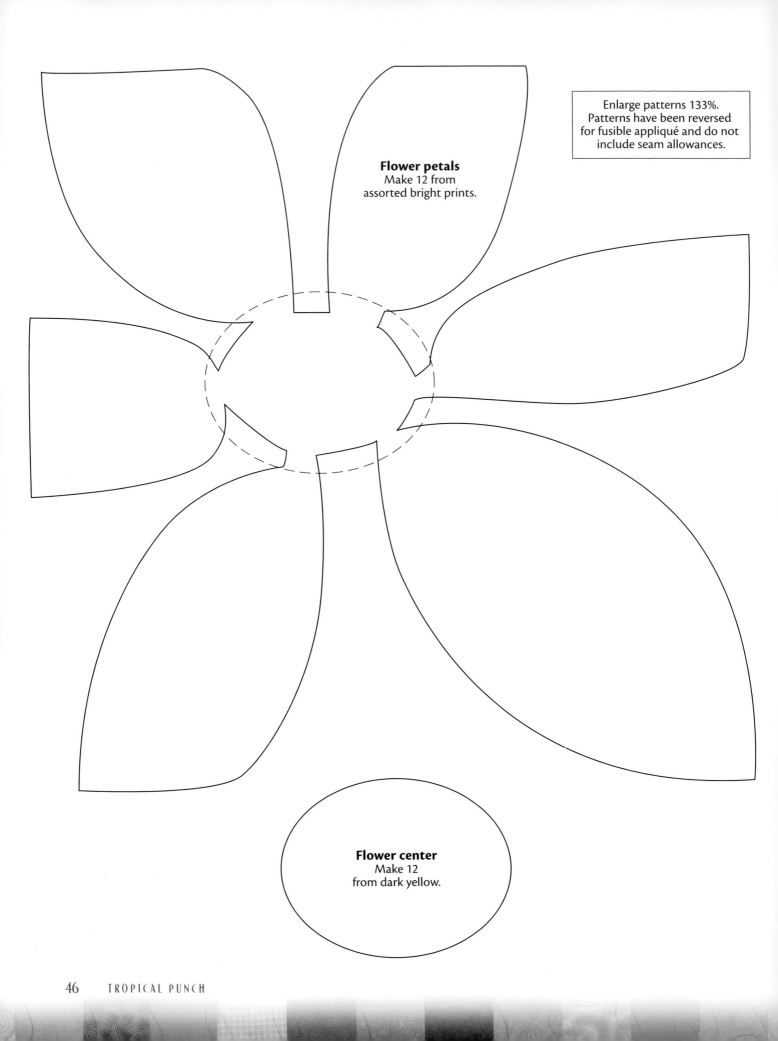

Flower petals
Make 12 from
assorted bright prints.

Enlarge patterns 133%.
Patterns have been reversed
for fusible appliqué and do not
include seam allowances.

Flower center
Make 12
from dark yellow.

LABYRINTH

Pieced by Tina Fonnesbeck and Julie Popa. Quilted by Paula Murray.

I love how this quilt turned out with a flea market–type look. To achieve this look, I had to stop trying to match all my fabrics and just go for it. Once I let go, it was quick and fun.

FINISHED QUILT: 64½" x 86"

Materials

Yardages are based on 42"-wide fabrics.
2⅝ yards *total* of assorted prints for pieced panels
1⅓ yards of red print for sashing and binding
1⅝ yards of brown solid for sashing
1⅓ yards of brown floral print for outer border
5⅝ yards of fabric for backing
72" x 93" piece of batting

Cutting

All measurements include ¼"-wide seam allowances. Cut all strips across the width of the fabric unless otherwise indicated.

From the assorted prints, cut a *total* of:
2 to 3 strips, 6½" wide, in various lengths to equal at least 60" long when pieced together
2 to 3 strips, 5½" wide, in various lengths to equal at least 60" long when pieced together
2 to 3 strips, 4½" wide, in various lengths to equal at least 60" long when pieced together
3½"-wide strips in various lengths to equal at least 300" long when pieced together
2½"-wide strips in various lengths to equal at least 360" long when pieced together

From the *lengthwise* grain of the brown solid, cut:
6 strips, 4½" x 50½"
5 rectangles, 4½" x 10"

From the red print, cut:
10 strips, 2" x 42"
8 strips, 2½" x 42"
5 rectangles, 4½" x 10"

From the brown floral, cut:
7 strips, 6" x 42"

Making the Pieced Panels

1. Sew several assorted print 2½"-wide strips of varied lengths together end to end to make a pieced strip 60" long, trimming the strip as needed to achieve the required length. Repeat with the remaining 2½"-wide strips to make a total of six pieced strips.

Make 6.

2. Repeat step 1 to make five 60"-long pieced strips from the 3½"-wide strips, and one 60"-long pieced strip *each* from the 4½"-, 5½"-, and 6½"-wide strips.

3. Sew the pieced strips together along the long edges in the order shown to make two strip sets, each measuring 21½" x 60". From the strip sets, cut a *total* of 10 segments, 10" wide.

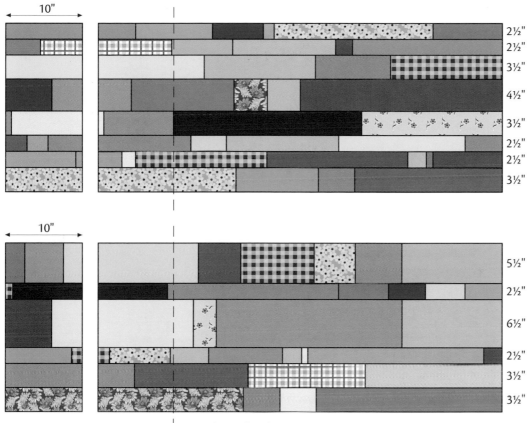

10"

2½"
2½"
3½"
4½"
3½"
2½"
2½"
3½"

10"

5½"
2½"
6½"
2½"
3½"
3½"

Make 1 of each strip set.
Cut 10 segments.

4. Arrange the segments into five rows of two segments each. Mix up the segments as much as possible by turning some of them upside down and/or moving them to opposite sides so that you spread out the colors across the quilt. When you are pleased with the arrangement, sew the segments in each row together.

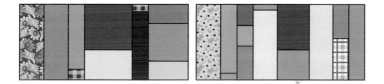

Assembling the Quilt Top

1. Refer to the quilt-assembly diagram to sew the red print and brown solid 4½" x 10" rectangles to the ends of the rows as shown. Press the seam allowances toward the rectangles. Sew the rows together, inserting a brown 4½" x 50½" sashing strip between each one. Press the seam allowances toward the sashing.

2. Sew the red 2" x 42" strips together and press the seam allowance to one side. Refer to "Adding Borders" on page 13 to cut and sew the middle border.

3. Repeat step 2 with the brown floral 6" x 42" strips to add the outer border.

Finishing the Quilt

Refer to "Finishing Techniques" on page 16 to layer and baste your quilt, and quilt as desired. Prepare the red binding and sew it to the quilt edges.

Quilt assembly

VERTIGO

By Julie Popa. Quilted by Paula Murray.

This fun, eye-catching quilt is made from two basic Nine Patch blocks, but it's hard to see where the blocks begin and end. If this color combination doesn't work for you, try one that does. You can't go wrong!

Finished Quilt: 66½" x 75½"
Finished Blocks 1 and 2: 9½" x 12½"
Finished Blocks 3 and 4: 9½" x 9½"

Materials

Yardages are based on 42"-wide fabrics.

2¼ yards *total* of assorted black prints and red prints for blocks

2 yards *total* of assorted white prints for blocks

1⅝ yards of red print for border

⅓ yard of white print 1 for blocks

¼ yard *each* of white print 4 and black prints 2 and 3 for blocks

⅛ yard *each* of white prints 2 and 3 and black prints 1 and 4 for blocks

⅔ yard of black print 5 for binding

5¼ yards of fabric for backing

76" x 86" piece of batting

Cutting

All measurements include ¼"-wide seam allowances.
Cut all strips across the width of the fabric.

From white print 1, cut:
2 strips, 1½" x 42"
24 rectangles, 1½" x 5"

From black print 1, cut:
1 strip, 3" x 42"

From white print 2, cut:
1 strip, 3" x 42"

From black print 2, cut:
2 strips, 1½" x 42"
18 rectangles, 1½" x 5"

From the assorted black prints and red prints, cut a *total* of:
24 rectangles, 4" x 5"
5 strips, 6" x 18"
8 strips, 4" x 18"
12 rectangles, 3" x 5"
8 strips, 3" x 18"
3 strips, 5" x 18"

From the assorted white prints, cut a *total* of:
18 rectangles, 4" x 5"
10 strips, 4" x 18"
4 strips, 6" x 18"
16 rectangles, 3" x 5"
4 strips, 5" x 18"
6 strips, 3" x 18"

From white print 3, cut:
1 strip, 3" x 42"

From black print 3, cut:
2 strips, 1½" x 42"
16 rectangles, 1½" x 5"

From white print 4, cut:
2 strips, 1½" x 42"
12 rectangles, 1½" x 5"

From black print 4, cut:
1 strip, 3" x 42"

From the red print for border, cut:
8 strips, 6½" x 42"

From black print 5, cut:
8 strips, 2½" x 42"

Making Blocks 1 and 2

1. Sew a 1½" x 42" white print 1 strip to the long edges of the 3" x 42" black print 1 strip to make strip set A. Press the seam allowances toward the black strip. Crosscut the strip set into 12 segments, 4" wide. Sew a 1½" x 42" black print 2 strip to the long edges of the 3" x 42" white print 2 strip to make strip set B. Press the seam allowances toward the black strips. Crosscut the strip set into 9 segments, 4" wide.

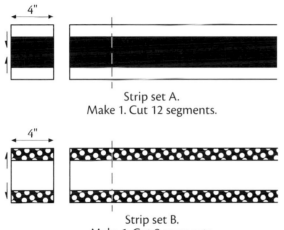

Strip set A.
Make 1. Cut 12 segments.

Strip set B.
Make 1. Cut 9 segments.

2. Add a 1½" x 5" white print 1 rectangle to the sides of each strip set A segment as shown to make unit A. Press the seam allowances toward the newly added rectangles. Make 12. In the same manner, join a 1½" x 5" black print 2 rectangle to the sides of each strip set B segment to make unit B. Press the seam allowances toward the newly added rectangles. Make 9.

Unit A.
Make 12.

Unit B.
Make 9.

3. Sew a 4" x 5" assorted red or black rectangle to the sides of each unit A. Press the seam allowances toward the rectangles. In the same manner, join a 4" x 5" assorted white rectangle to the sides of each unit B. Press the seam allowances toward the B units.

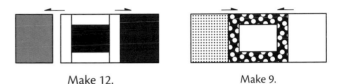

Make 12.   Make 9.

4. Sew a 4" x 18" assorted white strip to the long edges of a 6" x 18" assorted black or red strip to make strip set C. Make five. Press the seam allowances toward the red or black strips. Crosscut the strip sets into 24 segments, 3" wide. Sew a 4" x 18" assorted red or black strip to the long edges of a 6" x 18" assorted white strip to make strip set D. Make four. Press the seam allowances toward the red or black strips. Crosscut the strip sets into 18 segments, 3" wide.

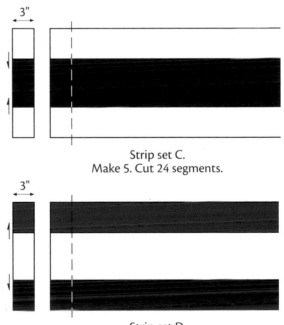

Strip set C.
Make 5. Cut 24 segments.

Strip set D.
Make 4. Cut 18 segments.

5. Add a strip set C segment to the top and bottom of each unit A from step 3 to complete block 1. Make 12. Join a strip set D segment to the top and bottom of each unit B from step 3 to complete block 2. Make 9. Press the seam allowances toward the strip-set segments.

Block 1.
Make 12.

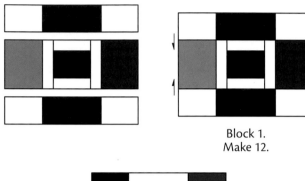

Block 2.
Make 9.

Making Blocks 3 and 4

1. Sew a 1½" x 42" black print 3 strip to the long edges of the 3" x 42" white print 3 strip to make strip set E. Press the seam allowances toward the black strips. Crosscut the strip set into eight segments, 3" wide.

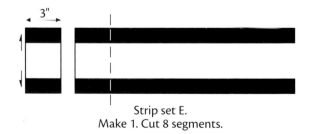

Strip set E.
Make 1. Cut 8 segments.

2. Sew a 1½" x 42" white print 4 strip to the long edges of the 3" x 42" black print 4 strip to make strip set F. Press the seam allowances toward the black strip. Crosscut the strip set into six segments, 3" wide.

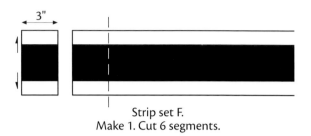

Strip set F.
Make 1. Cut 6 segments.

3. Add a 1½" x 5" black print 3 rectangle to the top and bottom of each strip set E segment as shown to make unit C. Make eight. In the same manner, join a 1½" x 5" white print 4 rectangle to the top and bottom of each strip set F segment to make unit D. Make six.

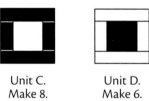

Unit C.
Make 8.

Unit D.
Make 6.

4. Sew a 3" x 5" assorted white rectangle to the sides of each unit C. Press the seam allowances toward the C units. In the same manner, join a 3" x 5" assorted black or red rectangle to the sides of each unit D. Press the seam allowances toward the rectangles.

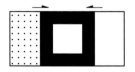

Make 8.

Make 6.

5. Sew a 3" x 18" assorted black or red strip to the long edges of a 5" x 18" assorted white strip to make strip set G. Make four. Press the seam allowances toward the red or black strips. Crosscut the strip sets into 16 segments, 3" wide.

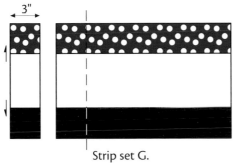

Strip set G.
Make 4. Cut 16 segments.

6. Sew a 3" x 18" assorted white strip to the long edges of a 5" x 18" assorted black or red strip to make strip set H. Make three. Press the seam allowances toward the red or black strips. Crosscut the strip sets into 12 segments, 3" wide.

Strip set H.
Make 3. Cut 12 segments.

7. Add a strip set G segment to the top and bottom of each unit C from step 4 to complete block 3. Make eight. Join a strip set H segment to the top and bottom of each unit D from step 4 to complete block 4. Make six. Press the seam allowances toward the C and D units.

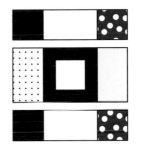 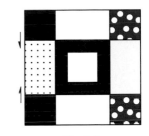

Block 3.
Make 8.

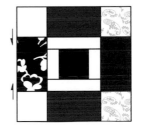

Block 4.
Make 6.

Assembling the Quilt Top

1. Arrange the blocks into seven horizontal rows as shown below. Be careful to position the blocks correctly within the rows. Rotate the blocks as needed to distribute the colors and create a pleasing layout. Sew the blocks into rows. Press the seam allowances in opposite directions from row to row. Sew the rows together. Press the seam allowances in one direction.

2. Sew the red print border strips together end to end and press the seam allowances to one side. Refer to "Adding Borders" on page 13 to cut and sew the border.

Finishing the Quilt

Refer to "Finishing Techniques" on page 16 to layer and baste your quilt, and quilt as desired. Prepare the black binding and sew it to the quilt edges.

ZigZag

By Julie Popa. Quilted by Paula Murray.

With its colors zigzagging in both directions, this bright quilt would be fun for anyone. If you like the look but prefer something more subdued, just use a calmer color palette.

FINISHED QUILT: 64½" x 82½"
FINISHED BLOCK: 9" x 9"

Materials

Yardages are based on 42"-wide fabrics.

2⅜ yards *total* of assorted dark blue prints for blocks

1¾ yards *total* of assorted yellow prints for blocks

1½ yards *total* of assorted red prints for blocks

1½ yards of dark blue for border

⅝ yard of red print for binding

4 yards of fabric for backing

72" x 90" piece of batting

Cutting

All measurements include ¼"-wide seam allowances. Cut all strips across the width of the fabric. Before you begin cutting, refer to "Making and Using Templates" on page 12 to make templates A and B from the patterns on page 60 and use them to cut out the indicated pieces.

From the assorted dark blue prints, cut a *total* of:
48 squares, 4½" x 4½"
48 template A pieces
48 template A reversed pieces

From the assorted red prints, cut a *total* of:
48 template A pieces
48 template A reversed pieces

From the assorted yellow prints, cut a *total* of:
96 template B pieces
96 template B reversed pieces

From the dark blue for border, cut:
8 strips, 5½" x 42"

From the red print for binding, cut:
8 strips, 2½" x 42"

Making the Blocks

1. Sew a dark blue template A piece to both sides of a dark blue 4½" square as shown. Press the seam allowances toward the square. Make 24 left-block center units. Repeat with the remaining squares and the template A reversed pieces to make 24 right-block center units.

 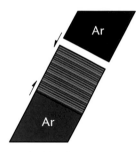

Left-block center unit.
Make 24.

Right-block center unit.
Make 24.

2. Sew a yellow template B piece to both sides of a red template A piece as shown. Press the seam allowances toward the template B pieces. Make 48 left-block side units.

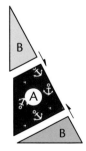

Left-block side unit.
Make 48.

3. Repeat step 2 with the red template A reversed pieces and the yellow template B reversed pieces. Make 48 right-block side units.

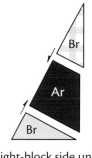

Right-block side unit.
Make 48.

4. Using the left-block units, sew a side unit to the sides of each center unit as shown, matching seams. Press the seam allowances toward the center units. Make 24.

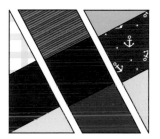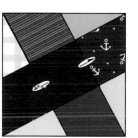

Left block.
Make 24.

5. Repeat step 3 with the right-block units to make 24 right blocks as shown. Press the seam allowances toward the side units.

Right block.
Make 24.

Assembling the Quilt Top

1. Lay out the blocks in eight rows of three left blocks and three right blocks each as shown. Alternate the blocks in each row and from row to row. Sew the blocks into rows. Press the seam allowances toward the left blocks. Sew the rows together. Press the seam allowances in either direction.

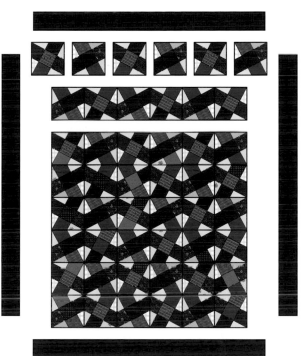

2. Sew the blue 5½" x 42" strips together end to end and press the seam allowances to one side. Refer to "Adding Borders" on page 13 to cut and sew the border.

Finishing the Quilt

Refer to "Finishing Techniques" on page 16 to layer and baste your quilt, and quilt as desired. Prepare the red binding and sew it to the quilt edge.

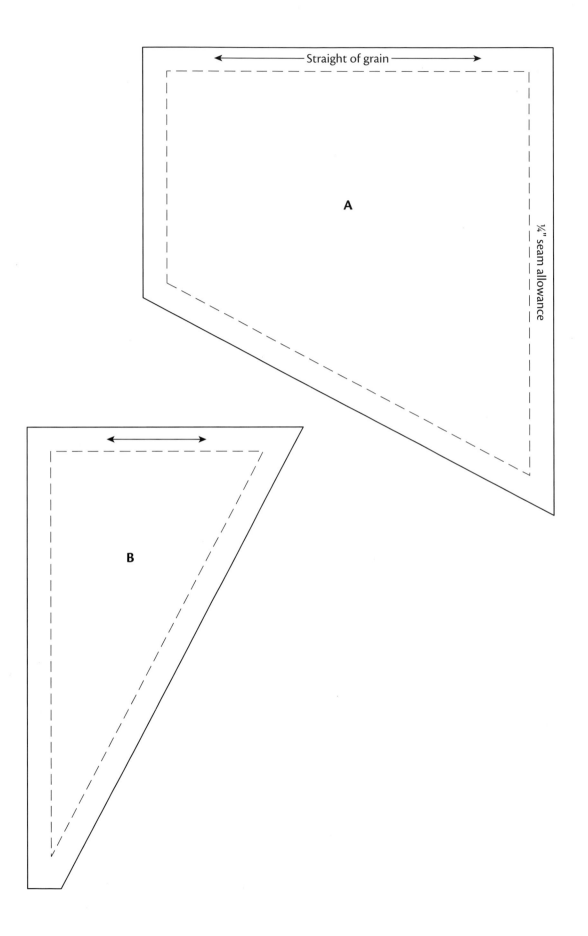

Straight of grain

A

¼" seam allowance

B

CHERRY BLOSSOMS

By Julie Popa. Quilted by Paula Murray.

Quilters of all ages will love the fun colors and funky prints used in this easy-to-make quilt. Even the appliqué goes quickly with the ease of fusible-web techniques.

FINISHED QUILT: 68½" x 79"

Materials

Yardages are based on 42"-wide fabrics.

2 yards of white print for appliqué-panel background

1¾ yards of large-scale floral print for border

1½ yards *total* of assorted pink prints for pieced panels and flower appliqués

⅔ yard of brown print for sashing and stem appliqué

⅝ yard *total* of assorted stripes and prints for pieced panels

½ yard *total* of assorted blue prints for pieced panels

⅜ yard of green print for pieced panels

Scraps of assorted green, pink, and orange prints for leaves and flower centers

⅔ yard of pink print for binding

5¼ yards of fabric for backing

77" x 86" piece of batting

3 yards of 17"-wide paper-backed fusible web

Cutting

All measurements include ¼"-wide seam allowances. Cut all strips across the width of the fabric unless otherwise indicated.

From the assorted pink prints, cut a *total* of:
3 strips, 6" x 42"
3 strips, 4" x 42"
1 strip, 2" x 42"

From the assorted blue prints, cut a *total* of:
2 strips, 4" x 42"
2 strips, 2" x 42"

From the green print, cut:
2 strips, 4" x 42"
1 strip, 2" x 42"

From the assorted stripes and prints, cut a *total* of:
3 strips, 6" x 42"

From the *lengthwise* grain of the white print, cut:
1 strip, 14½" x 64"

From the brown print, cut:
4 strips, 2½" x 42"

From the large-scale floral print, cut:
7 strips, 8" x 42"

From the pink print for binding, cut:
8 strips, 2½" x 42"

Making the Panels

1. To make the appliquéd panel, use the patterns on page 65 and refer to "Fusible-Web Appliqué" on page 14 to make the appliqués from the fabric specified on the patterns, trimming away the excess fusible web from the fusible-web flower shapes before adhering them to the assorted pink fabrics.

2. Arrange the appliqués on the white strip as shown, beginning with the stems. Follow the manufacturer's instructions to fuse the appliqués in place.

3. Machine blanket-stitch around the edges of the appliqué shapes to secure them in place.

4. To make the pieced panels, sew the assorted pink, blue, green, stripe, and print 42"-long strips together along the long edges in the order shown. (Do not include the brown strips.) Press the seam allowances in one direction. The strip set should measure 64" long. If it does not, take in or let out one or more seam allowances to achieve the correct length. Crosscut the strip set into one panel, 26½" wide, and one panel, 9½" wide.

9½"   26½"

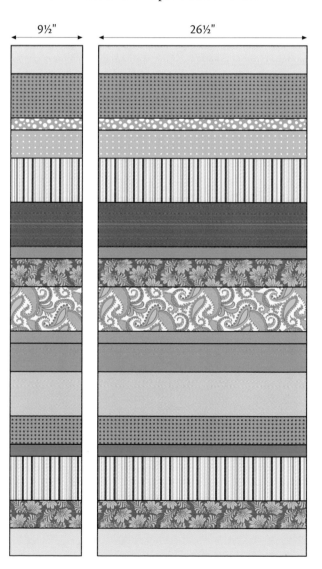

Assembling the Quilt Top

1. Join two brown 2½" x 42" strips together end to end to make one long strip. Repeat with the remaining two strips. Trim the strips to 64" long. Sew the strips to the long edges of the appliquéd panel. Press the seam allowances toward the brown strips.

2. Sew the pieced panels to the long edges of the appliquéd panel as shown. Press the seam allowances toward the brown strips.

3. Refer to "Adding Borders" on page 13 to trim the large-scale floral strips to the lengths needed for the border and sew them to the quilt top. Press the seam allowances toward the border.

Finishing the Quilt

Refer to "Finishing Techniques" on page 16 to layer and baste your quilt, and quilt as desired. Prepare the pink binding and sew it to the quilt edges.

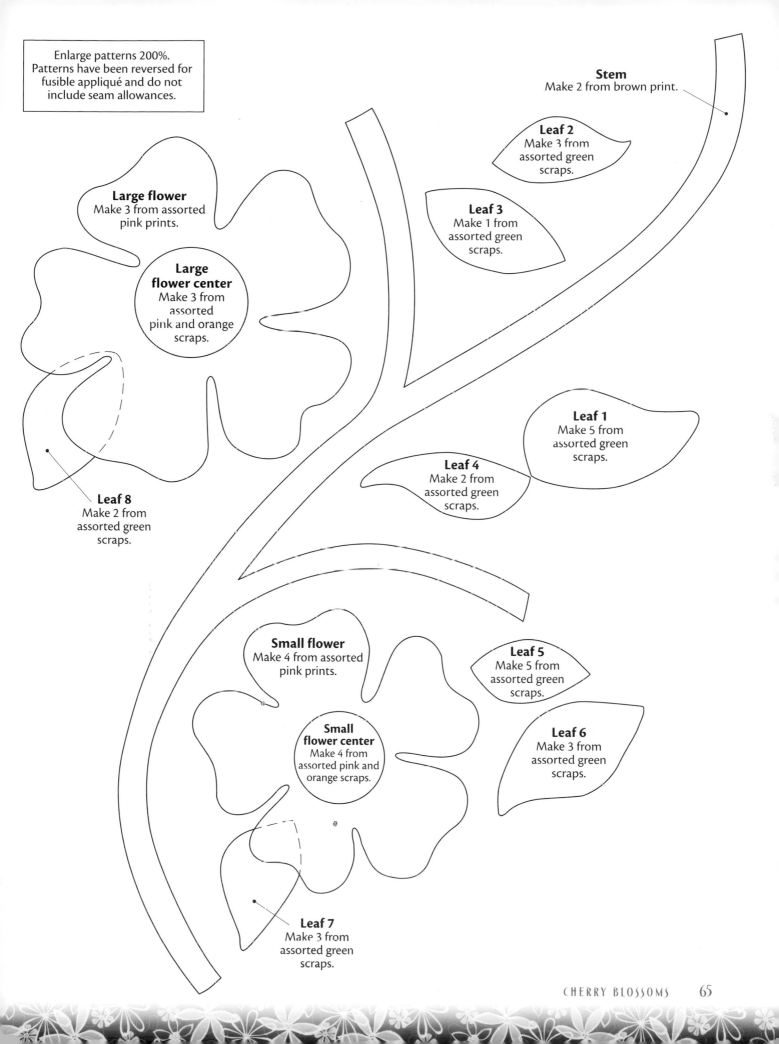

Enlarge patterns 200%. Patterns have been reversed for fusible appliqué and do not include seam allowances.

Stem
Make 2 from brown print.

Leaf 2
Make 3 from assorted green scraps.

Leaf 3
Make 1 from assorted green scraps.

Large flower
Make 3 from assorted pink prints.

Large flower center
Make 3 from assorted pink and orange scraps.

Leaf 1
Make 5 from assorted green scraps.

Leaf 8
Make 2 from assorted green scraps.

Leaf 4
Make 2 from assorted green scraps.

Small flower
Make 4 from assorted pink prints.

Leaf 5
Make 5 from assorted green scraps.

Small flower center
Make 4 from assorted pink and orange scraps.

Leaf 6
Make 3 from assorted green scraps.

Leaf 7
Make 3 from assorted green scraps.

SECRET GARDEN

By Julie Popa. Quilted by Paula Murray.

Step into this secret garden filled with bright flowers and vines. The background of the quilt pieces together quickly, and fusible-appliqué techniques make this quilt easier than it looks.

Finished Quilt: 66⅜" x 88⅞"
Finished Block: 7" x 7"

Materials

Yardages are based on 42"-wide fabrics.

1⅓ yards *each* of 2 different green prints for vine and leaf appliqués

1⅞ yards of polka-dot print for blocks

1¾ yards of floral print for outer border

1½ yards of yellow print for sashing

1½ yards of white print for setting triangles and inner border

½ yard of reddish orange fabric for large outer-flower appliqués

½ yard *total* of assorted blue prints for small and medium flower appliqués

⅜ yard of tangerine print for middle border

¼ yard of dark red fabric for large inner-flower appliqués

⅛ yard of orange print for large flower-center appliqués

⅛ yard of light green for small and medium flower-center appliqués

¾ yard of red print for binding

5¾ yards of fabric for backing

72" x 94" piece of batting

7 yards of 17"-wide paper-backed fusible web

Cutting

All measurements include ¼"-wide seam allowances.
Cut all strips across the width of the fabric.

From the yellow print, cut:

46 rectangles, 2" x 7½"

2 rectangles, 2" x 9"

13 strips, 2" x 42"; crosscut 4 strips into:
- 2 strips, 2" x 22"
- 2 strips, 2" x 39"

From the polka-dot print, cut:

38 squares, 7½" x 7½"

From the white print, cut:

5 squares, 11⅛" x 11⅛"; cut twice diagonally to yield 20 setting triangles

8 strips, 3" x 42"

From the tangerine print, cut:

8 strips, 1¼" x 42"

From the floral print, cut:

8 strips, 7" x 42"

From the red print, cut:

9 strips, 2½" x 42"

Assembling the Quilt Top

1. Sew the nine yellow 2" x 42" strips together end to end to make one long strip. Press the seam allowances to one side. From the pieced strip, cut three strips, 2" x 72", and two strips, 2" x 56".

2. Refer to the quilt diagram to lay out and arrange the polka-dot squares, white triangles, and yellow sashing rectangles and strips into diagonal rows as shown.

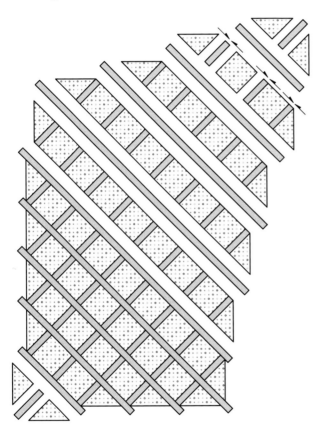

3. Sew the squares, setting triangles, and sashing rectangles of each block row together first. Press the seam allowances toward the sashing. Lay the assembled block rows in the proper order.

4. Sew the setting triangles and yellow 2" x 9" sashing rectangles in the upper-right corner and lower-left corner together, keeping the lower edges even. The sashing will extend above the triangle points. Trim the sashing even with the setting-triangle edges as shown. Lay the assembled corners in place.

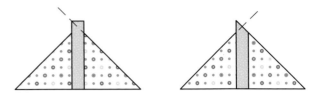

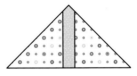

5. Sew the block rows and yellow sashing strips together in the order shown, matching the seams of the 2" x 7½" sashing rectangles between rows. The sashing strips are cut longer than necessary and should extend beyond the ends of the rows. Press the seam allowances toward the sashing strips. Trim the sashing that extends beyond the quilt top even with the setting triangles.

6. Sew the white 3" x 42" strips together end to end and press the seam allowances to one side. Refer to "Adding Borders" on page 13 to cut and sew the inner border. Repeat with the tangerine strips to add the middle border.

7. Using the patterns on pages 70–71, refer to "Fusible-Web Appliqué" on page 14 to make the appliqués from the fabrics specified on the patterns, trimming away the excess fusible web from the center of the fusible-web large flower shapes before adhering them to the reddish orange and dark red fabrics.

8. Position the vines and then the flowers on the pieced background as shown below. Use the large flowers and double leaves to cover the vine ends that do not quite meet.

9. Using a machine blanket stitch or zigzag stitch, stitch around the edges of the appliqué shape to secure them in place.

10. Sew the floral-print strips together end to end and press the seam allowances to one side. Refer to "Adding Borders" to cut and sew the outer border.

Finishing the Quilt

Refer to "Finishing Techniques" on page 16 to layer and baste your quilt, and quilt as desired. Prepare the red binding and sew it to the quilt edges.

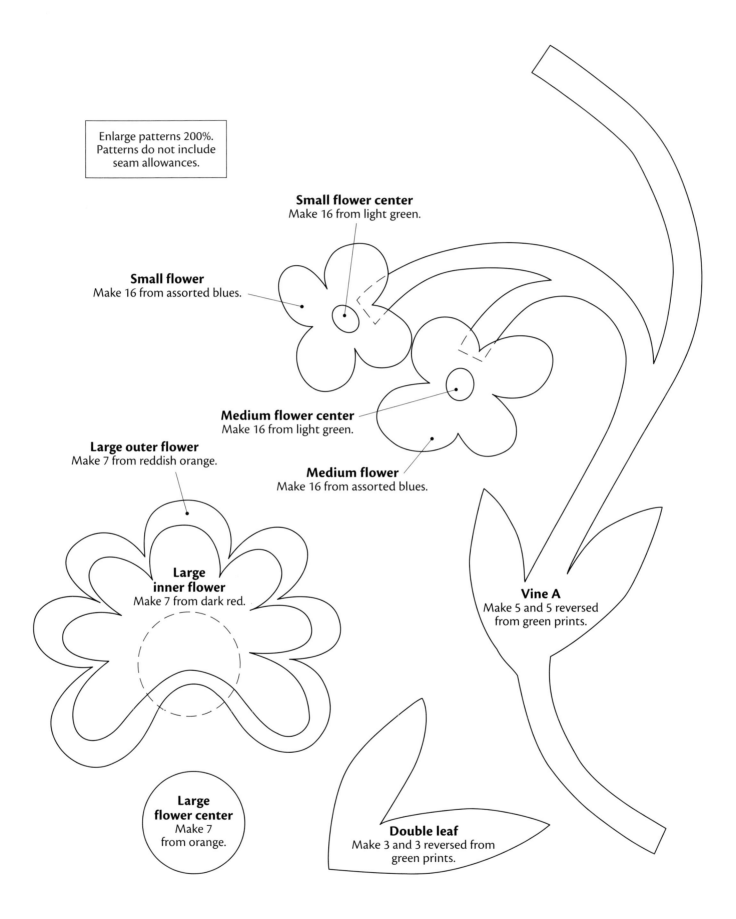

Enlarge patterns 200%.
Patterns do not include
seam allowances.

Small flower center
Make 16 from light green.

Small flower
Make 16 from assorted blues.

Medium flower center
Make 16 from light green.

Medium flower
Make 16 from assorted blues.

Large outer flower
Make 7 from reddish orange.

**Large
inner flower**
Make 7 from dark red.

Vine A
Make 5 and 5 reversed
from green prints.

**Large
flower center**
Make 7
from orange.

Double leaf
Make 3 and 3 reversed from
green prints.

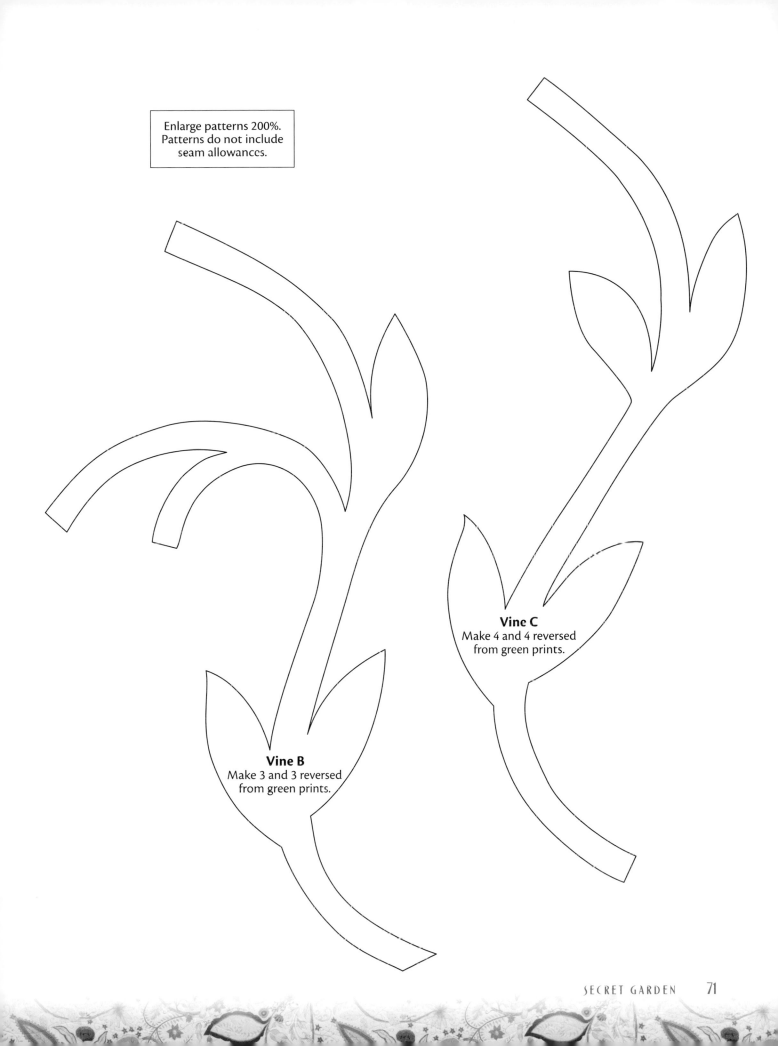

Enlarge patterns 200%.
Patterns do not include
seam allowances.

Vine C
Make 4 and 4 reversed
from green prints.

Vine B
Make 3 and 3 reversed
from green prints.

CITY STREETS

By Julie Popa. Quilted by Paula Murray.

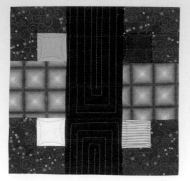

This quilt makes a great gift for a son, grandson, or other special guy in your life. The simple design makes the project easy to complete in a weekend.

FINISHED QUILT: 57½" x 69½"
FINISHED BLOCK: 12" x 12"

Materials

Yardages are based on 42"-wide fabrics.

2⅓ yards of black print for blocks and border

1 yard of blue solid for blocks

½ yard of blue print for blocks

⅝ yard *total* of assorted red, yellow, and white solids for blocks

⅝ yard of gray print for blocks

⅝ yards of black-and-white print for binding

4 yards of fabric for backing

65" x 77" piece of batting

Cutting

All measurements include ¼"-wide seam allowances.
Cut all strips across the width of the fabric.

From the assorted red, yellow, and white solids, cut a *total* of:

80 squares, 2½" x 2½"

From the blue solid, cut:

56 squares, 2½" x 2½"

56 rectangles, 2½" x 4½"

From the blue print, cut:

24 squares, 2½" x 2½"

24 rectangles, 2½" x 4½"

From the black print, cut:

14 rectangles, 4½" x 12½"

28 squares, 4½" x 4½"

7 strips, 5" x 42"

From the gray print, cut:

6 rectangles, 4½" x 12½"

12 squares, 4½" x 4½"

From the black-and-white print, cut:

7 strips, 2½" x 42"

Making the Blocks

1. Sew each assorted red, yellow, and white 2½" square to a blue solid or blue print 2½" square. Make a total of 80 units. Press the seam allowances toward the blue squares.

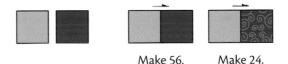

Make 56.   Make 24.

2. Sew the blue solid 2½" x 4½" rectangles to each step 1 unit with a blue solid square as shown. Repeat with the blue print rectangles and the remaining step 1 units. Press the seam allowances toward the rectangles.

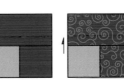

Make 56.   Make 24.

3. Sew the step 2 units and the black print and gray print 4½" squares together to make the units shown. Make the number indicated for each combination. Press the seam allowances toward the squares.

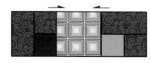

Make 28. Make 12.

4. Sew the step 3 units to the long edges of the black print and gray print 4½" x 12½" rectangles to make the block combinations shown. Make the number indicated for each combination. Press the seam allowances toward the rectangles.

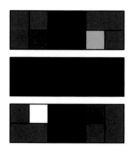

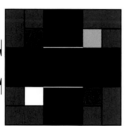

Make 8.

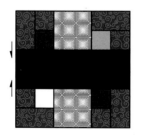

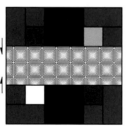

Make 6. Make 6.

Assembling the Quilt Top

1. Arrange the blocks in five horizontal rows of four blocks each as shown. Be careful to place the correct block in each position, rotating it as needed. Sew the blocks into rows. Press the seam allowances in opposite directions from row to row. Sew the rows together. Press the seam allowances in either direction.

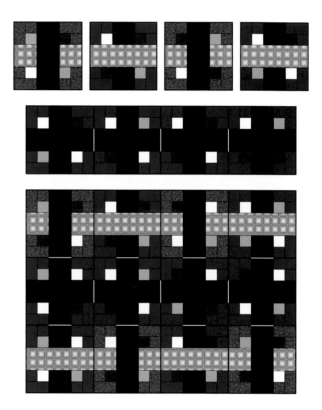

2. Sew the black print 5" x 42" strips together end to end and press the seam allowances to one side. Refer to "Adding Borders" on page 13 to cut and sew the border.

Finishing the Quilt

Refer to "Finishing Techniques" on page 16 to layer and baste your quilt, and quilt as desired. Prepare the black-and-white binding and sew it to the quilt edges.

STARLIGHT

Pieced by Amanda Fonnesbeck, age 16, Nicole Fonnesbeck, age 15, and Julie Popa. Quilted by Paula Murray.

A whimsical quilt like this will brighten your daughter's room, and depending on her age and sewing skills, she could even help you make it. My teenage nieces chose the fabric and colors for this quilt and they also did the cutting and sewing of the individual blocks. It turned out to be a really fun quilt.

Finished Quilt: 71½" x 105½"
Finished Block: 16½" x 16½"

Materials

Yardages are based on 42"-wide fabrics.

¼ yard *each* of 12 different colored prints for pieced blocks and inner border

1⅞ yards of pink-and-red polka dot fabric for outer border

1⅞ yards of cream polka-dot fabric for blocks and inner border

1¾ yards of cream print for blocks and inner border

1⅝ yards of yellow print for star appliqués

⅞ yard of pink print for star appliqués

½ yard of medium lilac fabric for alternate block centers

½ yard of lime green fabric for alternate blocks and inner border

½ yard of medium purple fabric for swirl appliqués and inner border

⅞ yard of red print for binding

7 yards of fabric for backing

80" x 114" piece of batting

6⅓ yards of 17"-wide paper-backed fusible web

Cutting

All measurements include ¼"-wide seam allowances.
Cut all strips across the width of the fabric.

From the medium lilac, cut:
8 squares, 5¾" x 5¾"

From the lime green, cut:
16 squares, 4⅝" x 4⅝"; cut in half diagonally to yield 32 triangles
8 strips, 2" x 18"

From *each* of 8 of the different colored prints, cut:
2 strips, 2" x 18" (16 total)
12 rectangles, 2" x 5" (96 total)

From *each* of the remaining 4 different colored prints, cut:
8 rectangles, 2" x 8" (32 total)

From the cream polka-dot fabric, cut:
4 squares, 17" x 17"
4 rectangles, 5" x 17"
20 rectangles, 3½" x 8"

From the cream print, cut:
3 squares, 17" x 17"
6 rectangles, 5" x 17"
18 rectangles, 3½" x 8"

From the medium purple, cut:
6 rectangles, 2" x 8"

From the pink-and-red polka dot fabric, cut:
10 strips, 6" x 42"

From the red print, cut:
10 strips, 2½" x 42"

Making the Blocks

1. Sew a lime green triangle to opposite sides of each medium lilac square. Press the seam allowances toward the triangles. Repeat with the remaining sides. Make eight.

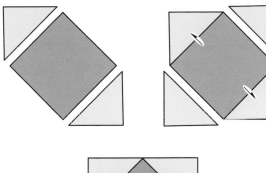

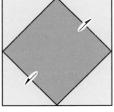

Make 8.

2. Sew four colored 2" x 8" rectangles of each of the four different colors to a cream polka-dot 3½" x 8" rectangle. Sew each of the remaining colored 2" x 8" rectangles to a cream print 3½" x 8" rectangle. Press the seam allowances toward the colored rectangles.

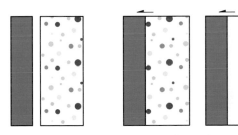

Make 4 of each
of 4 colors.

3. Sew two matching colored 2" x 18" strips to the long edges of a lime green 2" x 18" strip to make a strip set. Press the seam allowances away from the lime strip. Repeat to make a total of eight strip sets. Crosscut each strip set into six segments, 2" wide.

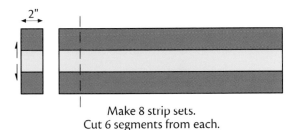

Make 8 strip sets.
Cut 6 segments from each.

4. Sew a matching 2" x 5" rectangle to the top and bottom of each strip-set segment as shown. Press the seam allowances toward the rectangles. Make a total of 48 units.

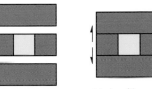

Make 48 total.

5. Arrange one step 1 unit, four matching step 2 units (two with cream polka-dot rectangles and two with cream print rectangles), and four step 4 units into three horizontal rows as shown on page 78. Sew the units in each row together. Press the seam allowances toward the step 2 units. Sew the rows together. Press the seam

allowances in one direction. Repeat to make a total of eight blocks. Set aside the remaining step 4 units for the inner border.

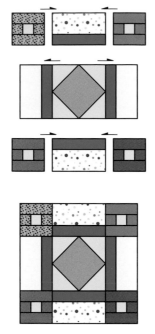

Make 8.

Assembling the Quilt Top

1. Sew the medium purple 2" x 8" rectangles to the remaining cream polka-dot and cream print 3½" x 8" rectangles as shown. Press the seam allowances toward the purple rectangles.

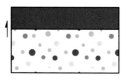

Make 4.

Make 2.

2. Lay out the pieced blocks, the cream print and cream polka-dot 17" squares, the cream print and cream polka-dot 5" x 17" rectangles, the remaining pieced squares from step 4 of "Making the Blocks," and the units from step 1 into seven horizontal rows as shown. Be careful to orient the pieced blocks so the cream polka-dot and cream print rectangles are in the correct positions. Sew the units into rows. Press the seam allowances in the directions indicated. Sew the rows together. Press the seam allowances in either direction.

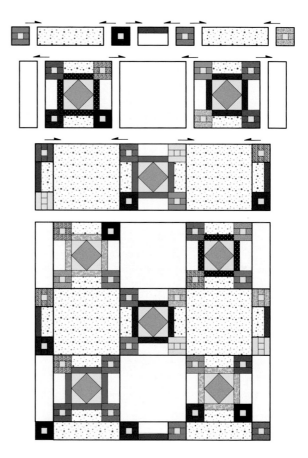

3. Using the patterns on page 80, refer to "Fusible-Web Appliqué" on page 14 to make the appliqués from fabrics specified on the patterns, trimming away the excess fusible web from the center of the fusible-web star shapes before adhering them to the pink and yellow fabrics.

4. Position the appliqués on the cream print and cream polka-dot 17" squares as shown. Follow the manufacturer's instructions to fuse the appliqués in place.

5. Machine zigzag stitch around the edges of the appliqué shapes to secure them in place.

6. Sew the pink-and-red polka-dot strips together end to end and press the seam allowances to one side. Refer to "Adding Borders" on page 13 to cut and sew the border.

Finishing the Quilt

Refer to "Finishing Techniques" on page 16 to layer and baste your quilt, and quilt as desired. Prepare the red binding and sew it to the quilt edges.

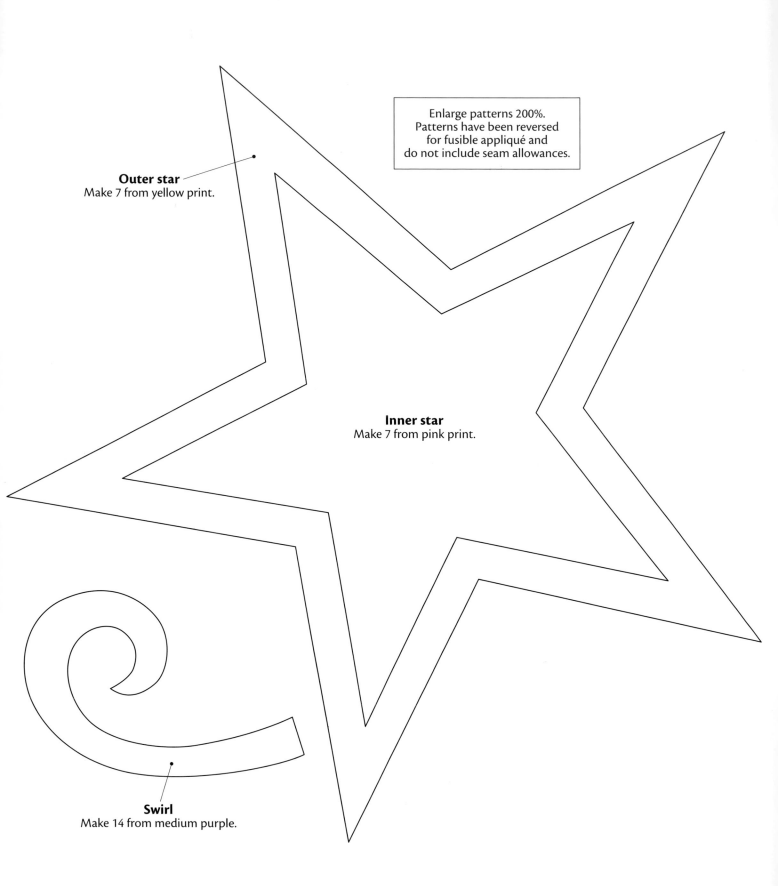

Outer star
Make 7 from yellow print.

Enlarge patterns 200%.
Patterns have been reversed
for fusible appliqué and
do not include seam allowances.

Inner star
Make 7 from pink print.

Swirl
Make 14 from medium purple.

TWIST AND TURN

By Julie Popa. Quilted by Paula Murray.

I like to pick a theme for each quilt to help me stay consistent with the colors and fabric choices. Some themes are very subtle, like this one. For the creams, I chose anything that reminded me of the beach; the blues were for the sky and water. The blocks in this quilt are surprisingly easy to make, and their large size creates a sizable quilt in no time.

FINISHED QUILT: 58½" x 73½"
FINISHED BLOCK: 15" x 15"

Materials

Yardages are based on 42"-wide fabrics.
1½ yards of very dark blue plaid for border
1⅓ yards *total* of assorted cream prints for blocks
⅔ yard *each* of 2 different dark blue prints for blocks
½ yard *each* of 1 medium blue print and 1 light blue print for blocks
⅝ yard of medium blue print for binding
4 yards of fabric for backing
66" x 81" piece of batting

Cutting

All measurements include ¼"-wide seam allowances. Cut all strips across the width of the fabric.

From the assorted cream prints, cut 24 matching sets consisting of:
1 square, 5⅛" x 5⅛" (24 total); cut in half diagonally to yield 2 half-square triangles (48 total)
1 square, 5½" x 5½" (24 total); cut twice diagonally to yield 4 quarter-square triangles (96 total)

From *each* of the medium blue and light blue prints, cut:
24 rectangles, 3½" x 6½" (48 total)

From *each* of the dark blue prints for blocks, cut:
24 rectangles, 2⅝" x 11½" (48 total)

From the very dark blue plaid, cut:
7 strips, 7" x 42"

From the medium blue print for binding, cut:
7 strips, 2½" x 42"

Making the Blocks

1. Sew two matching cream quarter-square triangles to the short sides of a medium or light blue 3½" x 6½" rectangle as shown. Press the seam allowances toward the triangles. Make one additional unit using the same color combination. Repeat to make a total of 12 pairs of light blue units and 12 pairs of medium blue units (48 total).

Make 12 pairs.

Make 12 pairs.

2. Sew a matching cream half-square triangle to each step 1 unit as shown. Press the seam allowances toward the half-square triangles. Make a total of 48 units.

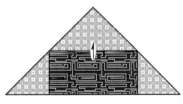

Make 48.

3. Sew matching dark blue 2⅝" x 11½" rectangles to each medium blue triangle unit from step 2, aligning the top of the strip with the left edge of the unit as shown. Press the seam allowances toward the rectangles. Repeat to sew the remaining dark blue rectangles to the light blue units from step 2. Trim the ends

of the rectangles even with the bottom of the triangle units. Make a total of 48 units.

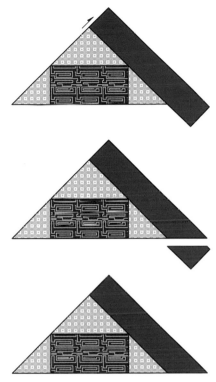

Make 48.

4. Sew two matching medium blue units and two matching light blue units from step 3 together as shown. Press the seam allowances in the directions indicated. Make 12 blocks.

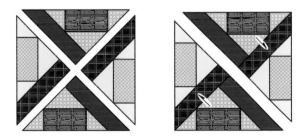

Make 12.

Assembling the Quilt Top

1. Arrange the blocks in four horizontal rows of three blocks each as shown below. Sew the blocks into rows. Press the seam allowances in opposite directions from row to row. Sew the rows together. Press the seam allowances in either direction.

2. Sew the plaid 7" x 42" strips together end to end and press the seam allowances to one side. Refer to "Adding Borders" on page 13 to cut and sew the border.

Finishing the Quilt

Refer to "Finishing Techniques" on page 16 to layer and baste your quilt, and quilt as desired. Prepare the medium blue binding and sew it to the quilt edges.

REFLECTION

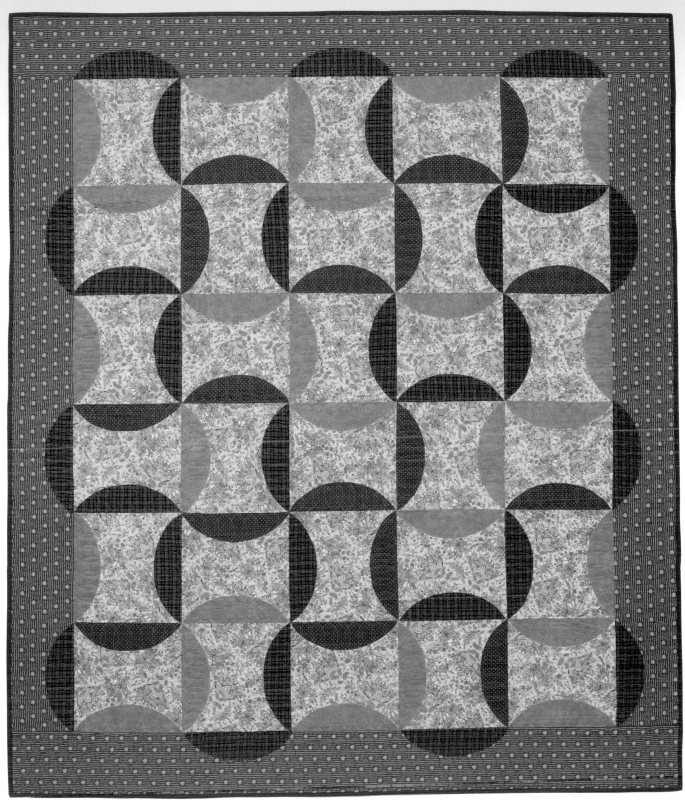

By Julie Popa. Quilted by Paula Murray.

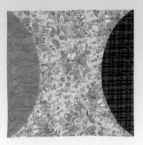

The scallops on this quilt are machine appliquéd to make this quilt easy to complete. Just choose a main print for the background squares and three coordinates to go with it for the scallops.

Finished Quilt: 68½" x 79½"
Finished Block: 11" x 11"

Materials

Yardages are based on 42"-wide fabrics.
3½ yards of floral print for blocks
1½ yards of brown polka-dot print for border
1⅓ yards of brown print for scallop appliqués and binding
1⅛ yards of pink print for scallop appliqués
1 yard of blue print for scallop appliqués
5⅓ yards of fabric for backing
76" x 87" piece of batting
5½ yards of 17"-wide paper-backed fusible web

Cutting

All measurements include ¼"-wide seam allowances.
Cut all strips across the width of the fabric.

From the floral print, cut:
30 squares, 11½" x 11½"

From the brown polka-dot print, cut:
7 strips, 7" x 42"

From the brown print for binding, cut:
8 strips, 2½" x 42"

Appliqué

1. Using the pattern on page 88, refer to "Fusible-Web Appliqué" on page 14 to make the appliqués from the fabrics specified on the pattern, trimming away the excess fusible web from the center of the fusible-web scallop shapes before adhering them to the fabrics.

2. Reeserve 11 pink scallops for the border. Randomly select two of the remaining appliqués and position them on opposite sides of a floral square. Align the appliqué straight edges with the square straight edges as shown. Follow the manufacturer's instructions to fuse the appliqués in place. Make 30.

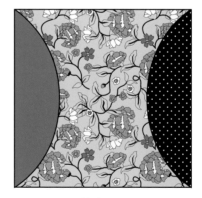

Make 30.

3. Machine blanket-stitch around the curved edges of the appliqué shapes to secure them in place.

4. Square up the blocks. Cut away the background fabric behind the scallops, leaving a ¼" seam allowance.

Assembling the Quilt Top

1. Arrange the blocks in six horizontal rows of five blocks each, rotating the blocks as shown to create the design. Sew the blocks into rows. Press the seam allowances in opposite directions from row to row. Sew the rows together. Press the seam allowances in either direction.

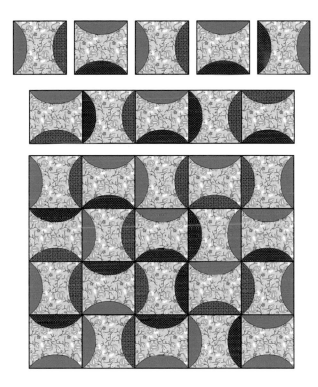

2. Refer to "Adding Borders" on page 13 to trim the brown polka-dot 7" x 42" strips to the lengths needed, but do not sew them to the quilt top yet. With right sides up, position the side borders along the sides of the quilt top, matching ends. Position three pink appliqués on each strip as shown. Fuse the appliqués in place. Machine blanket stitch around the curved edges of the appliqués. Sew the side borders to the sides of the quilt top. Press the seam allowances toward the border. Repeat with the top and bottom border strips, fusing three appliqués to the top border and two appliqués to the bottom border as shown.

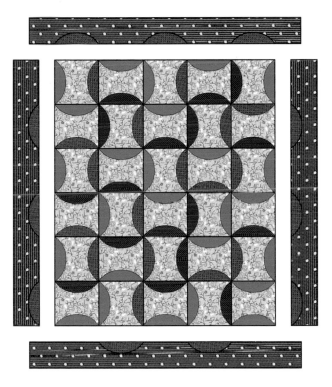

Finishing the Quilt

Refer to "Finishing Techniques" on page 16 to layer and baste your quilt, and quilt as desired. Prepare the brown binding and sew it to the quilt edges.

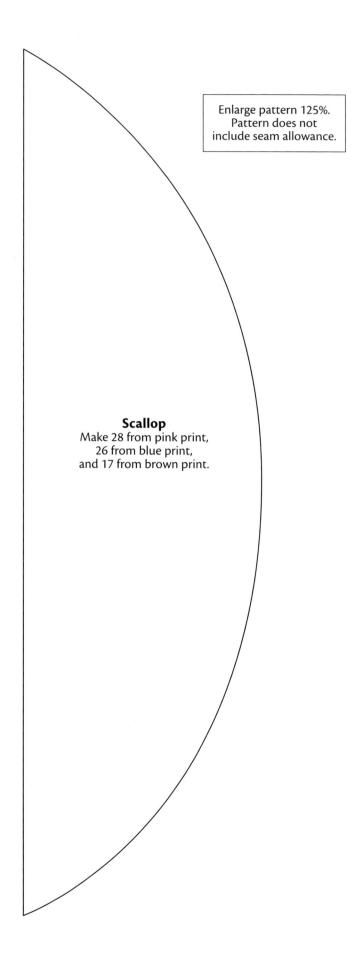

Enlarge pattern 125%.
Pattern does not
include seam allowance.

Scallop
Make 28 from pink print,
26 from blue print,
and 17 from brown print.

Katrina Murray, age 18, pieced the "Stripes" quilt (page 38) during a weekend home from college. It took her only about three hours to sew. Choosing fabric was especially fun because she was given free rein in her grandma's quilt shop.

Paula Murray liked "Twist and Turn" (page 81) because the block construction was unique and something new for her to piece. The yellow and pink made this a bright and splashy quilt for her daughter's bedroom.

Nicole Fonnesbeck, age 15, opted to make the "Labyrinth" quilt (page 47) because it looked easy. She enjoyed putting the fabrics together in random order. She chose the fabrics and colors because they looked grownup but still fun and bright. We lengthened and widened the pieced rows to fit a double bed.

Amanda Fonnesbeck, age 16, made this variation of the "Tropical Punch" quilt (page 42). She wanted hearts instead of flowers, so we changed the background block to a rectangle and modified the sashing and border sizes to fit her twin bed. She enjoyed seeing how the colors and fabrics she'd chosen came together to make such a fun quilt.

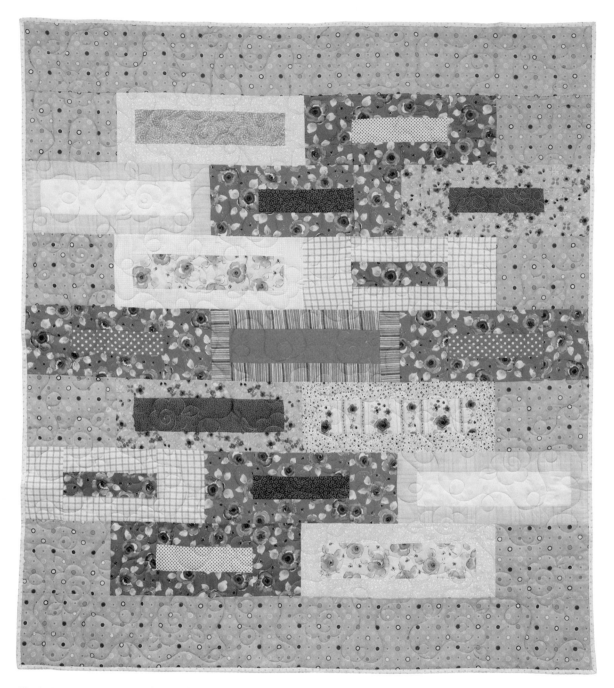

Alexis Popa, age 7, wanted to make the "Brickwork" quilt (page 29) because she loved its fun, scrappy style. We took out block B to make piecing easier for a beginner. She was excited about sewing each block, and she loved how the bright fabrics looked together.

Shanae Popa, age 10, enjoyed coordinating blue, green, and brown fabrics for this quilt. She used the "Cherry Blossoms" project (page 61), but decided to appliqué stars instead of flowers to fit her personality better. Sewing the strips together was easy, and she loves how it all turned out.

Tyler Fonnesbeck, age 12, really liked the "City Streets" quilt (page 72) and decided to make it for his new room. He chose yellow and black for his favorite college team, the Iowa Hawkeyes. He felt the quilt was easy to make with some help.

ABOUT THE AUTHOR

Julie Popa has been making quilts for many years and enjoys bringing her designs to life with a personality of their own. She received her BS in interior design in 1999 and enjoys incorporating those design principles into her quilts. She likes working with colors and continues to experiment with a variety of colors and prints to make each quilt unique. Julie founded Sunflower Hill Designs in 2001 to begin marketing her patterns. She resides in Smithfield, Utah, with her husband, Sean, and four children: Shanae, Alexis, Jaclyn, and Stockton.

NEW AND BESTSELLING TITLES FROM

Martingale®
& COMPANY

America's Best-Loved Craft & Hobby Books®
America's Best-Loved Knitting Books®

 That Patchwork Place®

America's Best-Loved Quilt Books®

APPLIQUÉ

Adoration Quilts
Appliqué at Play
Appliqué Takes Wing
Favorite Quilts from Anka's Treasures
Garden Party
Mimi Dietrich's Baltimore Basics
Stitch and Split Appliqué
Sunbonnet Sue and Scottie Too—*New!*
Tea in the Garden

FOCUS ON WOOL

Hooked on Wool
Needle Felting—*New!*
Simply Primitive

GENERAL QUILTMAKING

All Buttoned Up
Bound for Glory —*New!*
Calendar Kids
Colorful Quilts—*New!*
Creating Your Perfect Quilting Space
Creative Quilt Collection Volume Two
Dazzling Quilts
A Dozen Roses—*New!*
Follow-the-Line Quilting Designs
Follow-the-Line Quilting Designs
    Volume Two
A Fresh Look at Seasonal Quilts
Modern Primitive Quilts—*New!*
Positively Postcards—*New!*
Posterize It!—*New!*
Prairie Children and Their Quilts
Quilt Revival
Quilter's Block-a-Day Calendar—*New!*
Quilting in the Country—*New!*
Sensational Sashiko
Simple Traditions
Twice Quilted—*New!*

LEARNING TO QUILT

The Blessed Home Quilt
Color for the Terrified Quilter—*New!*
Happy Endings, Revised Edition
Let's Quilt!
The Magic of Quiltmaking
The Quilter's Quick Reference Guide
Your First Quilt Book (or it should be!)

PAPER PIECING

300 Paper-Pieced Quilt Blocks
Easy Machine Paper Piecing
Show Me How to Paper Piece
**Showstopping Quilts to Foundation
    Piece—*New!***
Spellbinding Quilts

PIECING

40 Fabulous Quick-Cut Quilts
Better by the Dozen
Big 'n Easy
Clever Quarters, Too
Lickety-Split Quilts
New Cuts for New Quilts
Over Easy
Sew One and You're Done
Snowball Quilts
Square Deal—*New!*
Stack a New Deck
Sudoku Quilts
Two-Block Theme Quilts
Twosey-Foursey Quilts
Wheel of Mystery Quilts

QUILTS FOR BABIES & CHILDREN

Even More Quilts for Baby
**The Little Box of Baby Quilts
    —*New!***
More Quilts for Baby
Quilts for Baby
Sweet and Simple Baby Quilts

SCRAP QUILTS

More Nickel Quilts
Nickel Quilts
Save the Scraps
Scraps of Time
Simple Strategies for Scrap Quilts
Successful Scrap Quilts from Simple
    Rectangles
A Treasury of Scrap Quilts

CRAFTS

Bag Boutique
Creative Embellishments—*New!*
Greeting Cards Using Digital Photos
It's a Wrap
**The Little Box of Beaded Bracelets
    and Earrings—*New!***
**The Little Box of Beaded Necklaces
    and Earrings—*New!***
Miniature Punchneedle Embroidery
A Passion for Punchneedle
Scrapbooking Off the Page...and on the Wall
Sculpted Threads—*New!*

KNITTING & CROCHET

365 Knitting Stitches a Year:
    Perpetual Calendar
A to Z of Knitting—*New!*
Crochet from the Heart
Crocheted Pursenalities—*New!*
First Crochet
First Knits
Fun and Funky Crochet
Funky Chunky Knitted Accessories
Handknit Style II
The Knitter's Book of Finishing
    Techniques
Knitting with Gigi—*New!*
The Little Box of Crochet for Baby—*New!*
The Little Box of Knitted Throws
Modern Classics
More Sensational Knitted Socks—*New!*
Pursenalities
Silk Knits
Top Down Sweaters—*New!*
Wrapped in Comfort—*New!*
The Yarn Stash Workbook

Our books are available at bookstores and your favorite craft, fabric,
and yarn retailers. If you don't see the title you're looking for,
visit us at **www.martingale-pub.com** or contact us at:

1-800-426-3126

International: 1-425-483-3313 • **Fax:** 1-425-486-7596 • **Email:** info@martingale-pub.com

3/07